ALBERT
SCHWEITZER

MODERN SPIRITUAL MASTERS
Robert Ellsberg, Series Editor

Already published:

MODERN SPIRITUAL MASTERS SERIES

ALBERT SCHWEITZER

Essential Writings

Selected with an Introduction by

JAMES BRABAZON

ORBIS BOOKS

Maryknoll, New York 10545

Founded in 1970, Orbis Books endeavors to publish works that enlighten the mind, nourish the spirit, and challenge the conscience. The publishing arm of the Maryknoll Fathers and Brothers, Orbis seeks to explore the global dimensions of the Christian faith and mission, to invite dialogue with diverse cultures and religious traditions, and to serve the cause of reconciliation and peace. The books published reflect the views of their authors and do not represent the official position of the Maryknoll Society. To learn more about Maryknoll and Orbis Books, please visit our website at www.maryknoll.org.

Grateful acknowledgement is made to Rhena Schweitzer Miller for permission to reprint these selections from her grandfather's writings.

Library of Congress Cataloging-in-Publication Data

Schweitzer, Albert, 1875-1965.
  [Selections. 2005]
  Albert Schweitzer : essential writings / selected with an introduction
by James Brabazon.
      p. cm. – (Modern spiritual masters series)
  ISBN-13: 978-1-57075-602-3 (pbk.)
  1. Theology. 2. Music. 3. Philosophy. I. Brabazon, James.
II. Title. III. Series.
BX4827.S35A25 2005
230 – dc22

2005008970

Contents

Foreword

Rhena Schweitzer-Miller

There have been several anthologies of quotations from my father's work and words. He was a highly quotable man. But most of the quotations were brief, designed to make an instant appeal to those who knew little of him and what he stood for.

This book goes further. The quotations are longer, doing justice to the range and depth of his thought, which often challenged accepted opinion, and the carefully presented arguments with which he backed up his challenges. This book is for those who are prepared to go with him into questions of life and belief that are profound, yet so simply and powerfully expressed that they can be easily followed.

I feel that the world needs his all-embracing philosophy of Reverence for Life more now than ever, and I hope that this book will bring many more people to adopt it and make it a foundation for their lives.

Introduction

Albert Schweitzer was a many-sided man, and in each of his sides he excelled. He earned degrees in theology, philosophy, music, and tropical medicine, and this at Strasbourg University, which at that time was at the hub of European intellectual life. He lived at a time when fresh discoveries about nature, about human psychology, about the universe, seemed to be leading to a wonderful new world of knowledge and the control of the world, and he was fully aware of all these developments. In his later years, while fully occupied with his jungle hospital, he studied the effects of fallout from hydrogen bombs and in three sensational worldwide broadcasts was the first to reveal to the world the horrors about to be unleashed.

But he insisted that such knowledge was not and could never be enough — for two reasons: first that life and the universe would always be beyond human comprehension; and second that knowledge was no use if it could not be put into practice for the benefit of all living creatures, for the enhancement of life and pleasure and the diminishment of pain. In a sermon he preached in 1902 he said, "Thought and analysis are powerless to pierce the great mystery that hovers over the world and over our existence, but knowledge of the great truths only appears in action and labor."

If Schweitzer had been content with the information then available, events would by now have left him far behind. The developments of quantum physics, of electronics, of communication and travel, have changed our world beyond recognition. But Schweitzer saw further and deeper. The things he studied — the life of Jesus, music, and the meaning of life itself — are everlasting, and his work on these may be disputed but can never be disregarded.

As a young man he was convinced that somewhere in the writings of the great theologians and philosophers there must be a concept that is universal, fundamental, elemental, to which he could give his assent, and he searched for it unceasingly.

Though his passion was driven by boundless energy, and all the surfaces of his room were covered with piles of books that he had read and were now gathering dust, he couldn't find it. It finally came to him not through books but through experience, in the heart of tropical Africa, and he called it Reverence for Life. If you dive deep down inside yourself, beyond the realm of reason (though not contrary to reason), you find solidarity with all of life. For him, the universe was made of life, and this was God. And to this he clung, in word and deed, all his life.

Deed was important. Not many thinkers and writers would be prepared to have their lives subjected to scrutiny on the basis of their pronouncements. But for Schweitzer this was crucial. "A man's life should be the same as his thought." "I have made my life my argument."

Albert Schweitzer's thinking was not that of a man who builds, but of a man who digs. In every area in which he worked he delved for the truth beneath the rubble and accretions of outdated theories and opinions received without thought. He did this with a rare combination of the passion of an artist and the ruthless rigor of a scholar.

And he was ruthless. He dispatched his opponents with a merciless efficiency that left them reeling, used as they were to the polite interchanges normal in academic discourse, which, however bitter, always left room for the dialogue to continue. Once Schweitzer had had his say, there was that terrible silence when somebody has said something shattering and unanswerable.

Indeed, distinguished academic as he was, he came to find academic discourse suffocating. As a teenager he had, on his own admission, become socially intolerable, through his insistence on asking awkward questions at friendly family gatherings. When his parents were invited to dinner, the invitation often included the instruction, "Don't bring Albert." This passionate search for truth made him a preeminent scholar in every field he touched — theology, philosophy, music — but in time these studies became inadequate for his ever-restless mind and spirit. He wrote to Hélène Bresslau, the woman who was to become his wife: "Today we had our Faculty meeting... when the program of courses was determined, I thought with a shudder that perhaps I might have spent my whole life preparing course schedules."

Finally, after months and years of searching for the spiritual satisfaction that eluded him, he knew that what he had to do was "something small in the spirit of Jesus."

By this time he knew something of the spirit of Jesus, because Jesus had been the subject of his most intense study and research — study that was far more than the analysis of texts, though that was an essential part of it: it was the imaginative penetration of a man into the mind of a man, who, though he might also be God, was also most essentially man.

Small indeed was the enterprise he embarked on in its beginnings: a converted chicken house on the grounds of a small mission settlement in the heart of tropical Africa, where he began to treat the natives for their multiple diseases, all complicated by malnutrition. But this small beginning grew, like the mustard seed in the parable, into a great tree that spread worldwide, and not only could the fowls of the air nest in it, but every living thing could find a sheltered place in its great shadow.

For it was here, surrounded by sickness and death, and nature at its cruelest as life fed indifferently on life, that the phrase "Reverence for Life" came to him. Nowhere else, he wrote to his daughter, Rhena, could he have found it.

In contrast to his published work I have inserted extracts from his ten-year correspondence with Hélène Bresslau before their marriage, in which the apparently assured outward man shows the emotional and intellectual furnace out of which he forged his convictions and determined the course of his life.

Given that emotional turmoil, perhaps as great as any of his achievements was one which by its very nature cannot appear in this book — his own personality. Forged by the fiery passion with which he approached life, and by the fierce self-discipline needed to control it, he was a formidable figure indeed. And yet those who met him — admittedly in his later years, because nobody is left who knew the younger man — speak of the immense kindliness, the twinkle in the clear, all-knowing eyes, and the sense he gave to everyone that he or she was the most important person in his world at that moment.

The passion, the brilliant intellect, and the concentration are clear enough from the extracts in this book. But I have not been able to show the charm and the humor and the great personal attractiveness to which all who knew him testified. Schweitzer was not only a great thinker, a prophet, and a dedicated humanitarian — he was a complete and very human man. If you want one phrase to sum him up, says his daughter, it was sex appeal.

To those who have perhaps had an easier path to their beliefs and who may think that his lack of orthodoxy and the conflicting passions that he admits to invalidate his conclusions, I would only say: How many Christian believers do you know who have followed such a simple, Christlike life in the steps of their Master?

•

Albert Schweitzer was born in Alsace, a region where dramatic mountains and quiet valleys sweep down to the plains that border the Rhine — a region that produces good timber and excellent wine. He liked to remark that the year of his birth, 1875, was a fine vintage year.

Germany had just defeated France in the Franco-Prussian War, and Alsace, which lies between the two powerful neighbors, was, as usual, claimed by the victors as part of the spoils of war. So Schweitzer might have been French had the war gone the other way, but in fact was born German. The Alsatians were bilingual and his parents' house was full of books in both German and French. But this accident of history was to cause him great problems later.

The son of a Lutheran village pastor, reared in one of the serene valleys of the Vosges, from early childhood Schweitzer was acutely sensitive to nature, and especially to the suffering of animals. He was also aware of violence in himself, which led to fierce inner conflicts.

Throughout his teens he was a great nuisance to his relatives, through his constant questioning of everything the grown-ups told him. He was tormented by questions: Where does pain come from? Why is it necessary? And what philosophy or religion could explain it and give the world a true ethical basis for dealing with it?

He was a hopeless dunce at school until he saw the point of study. But later his passionate questioning made of him a brilliant scholar, as he searched the books of great philosophers and theologians for the answers to his problems. Yet he never found what he was looking for. His frustrated quest for truth led him to something like a nervous breakdown, and at the age of twenty-one he decided that no amount of study would take away "the pain of the world's pain." He could live with himself only if he made a vow that at the age of thirty he would dedicate himself to some kind of practical work to alleviate suffering.

To everything that he touched he gave a fierce intellectual passion. Music was one such passion. Something of a child prodigy on the piano, he developed a love of the great organs of the churches of Strasbourg and Colmar. For relaxation he loved to play the piano at dances in the mountain inns. He slept very little, having the physique of a bull to keep him going. His energy and good looks made him very popular with the girls, though he had little time to spare for romance.

He earned a living as assistant pastor, in his sermons striving always to talk about the truth of lived experience, not pious theory. The sermons were simple, powerful, and very popular.

And still he searched for the fundamental truth he felt had been missed. At Strasbourg University he would sit up all night with his feet in cold water, reading and scribbling notes. It was a time when the intellectual world of Europe — and Strasbourg was very much a center of that world — was bubbling with the new ideas of Marx, Freud, and Nietzsche. Schweitzer was almost alone mistrusting them, for he saw how they were eroding individual humanity. He foresaw the mass movements that were to tear Europe apart.

Not the least of his passions was the figure of Jesus. Studying the Gospels with his usual combination of scholarship and insight, he found puzzles that he felt had been ignored by biblical scholars hitherto, and he began to dig for the truth of "the historical Jesus." The conclusions that he found forced upon him ran counter to the views accepted by all his colleagues and indeed the whole Christian community. His devotion to the person of Jesus, however, became his permanent inspiration. His theological views, then so startling, are now accepted by many serious biblical scholars.

By now he was becoming famous as a theologian, a philosopher, and a musician, earning degrees in all three fields. He loved his life in the church as pastor/preacher, in the university with its intellectual cut and thrust, and as a child of the Alsatian countryside, but he held to his resolution that at the age of thirty he would abandon all that and do "something small in the spirit of Jesus," though he didn't know what.

When he was thirty a chance article in a magazine made up his mind for him: doctors were needed at the Lambaréné Mission on the Ogowe River, in the French colony of the Gabon in Central Africa. Schweitzer was deeply aware of the damage that white men had done on that continent, and this was a chance to pay back a very small part of that debt. He would become a student all over again, this time learning tropical medicine, while still lecturing in theology and philosophy.

It took seven years. When he was qualified, he went to the Paris Missionary Society and offered his services. They refused him. Despite his lifelong devotion to Jesus, no missionary society would support him: his theological views were too unorthodox.

Controlling his quick temper, he decided that he alone would raise all the money he needed for his project. He begged, and he gave organ recitals, and slowly the money came in.

He was not quite alone. One of the young women who surrounded him, Hélène Bresslau, helped him with the fund-raising and adapted her medical training so as to go with him as a nurse. Schweitzer was delighted. Hélène's parents less so. They could never allow their daughter to go into the jungle with this very masculine young man unless he married her.

So they got married. It was not a love-match, at least not on his side. It was an arrangement by which two people, both dedicated to a single cause, could work together.

It was 1913 by the time they were ready to go to Africa. War clouds were gathering. As German citizens working in a French colony the Schweitzers were risking more than the usual tropical diseases.

But the diseases were real enough. The normal life expectation of white men and women on the Ogowe was five years. They were going on what was almost a suicide mission for the sake of the sick Africans.

The mission station of Lambaréné is 150 miles up river from the coast and the capital. There were no roads, and the only way to reach the mission was by river steamer and canoe. Once there, they had not only to heal but to build their hospital at the same time. Only Schweitzer's rugged constitution could have stood up to it. And once World War I started they were unable to get back home for a very necessary rest.

They treated every tropical disease, often several diseases in one patient. Many of the cases required surgery. Schweitzer was an extremely proficient doctor and surgeon.

It was here, among the sick Africans, in the savage and unforgiving jungle, where every creature and every plant preyed on another, that the words came to Schweitzer — "Reverence for Life": the answer to his questions, the basic philosophy that included all living things. "I am life, that wills to live, in the midst of life that wills to live." Very simple, its truth self-evident. But it had never been stated before as a serious philosophy nor its implications examined.

After four years, their hospital was still growing. Then they were arrested. Technically they were enemy aliens, despite the work they were doing. The authorities were appealed to but would not listen. They were taken to France and interned in an old monastery in the Pyrenees. It was bitterly cold, their blood was thinned by tropical heat, and they had no winter clothes. Hélène suffered a recurrence of tuberculosis, believed cleared before the war. And it was here that she became pregnant.

Important people interceded for them, and finally they went home to Alsace. It was unrecognizable. Savage battles had been fought over their homeland; the country was laid waste and towns shattered. Sick, tired, penniless, and with a child on the way, they had to pick up their lives from nothing. For Schweitzer's name no longer meant anything in the university. There were new people in charge. He was lucky to get a job as an assistant curate.

Slowly they got well. Schweitzer lectured on Reverence for Life, showing that it crossed all barriers, not only between human beings but between humans and animals. Many people already lived with this sense of the value of life. Now there was a philosophy to support their instinctive humanity.

Hélène never fully recovered from tuberculosis. And when the moment came that Schweitzer had again collected enough money to go back to Africa and pick up their dream where it had been interrupted, they had to face the fact that she was no longer the strong woman who had set out in 1913. And there was their daughter, Rhena: to leave her behind was out of the question, nor could they risk her health in the Gabon. Hélène accepted the parting, but it was a bitter situation and remained so for the rest of their lives.

When Schweitzer returned to Lambaréné, the hospital they had built no longer existed. Termites had eaten it; undergrowth had covered it. After a brief attempt to resurrect it, Schweitzer decided to start again, a few miles up river, where there was more room and more air.

He cut down the trees, sawed them up, shaped the timbers, designed the buildings, and built them. His helpers were the walking wounded, the less sick patients. He was fifty. For the next forty years his permanent home was to be the tiny room in the hospital — barely big enough for a bed and a desk and a wash basin.

And here he fought to preserve his vision, to keep the place simple and homely. Reverence for Life meant that every creature was welcome. And this had a practical side. (Schweitzer always claimed, as we are gradually discovering many years later, that doing the right thing is also doing the sensible thing.) The animals dropped dung. Dung fertilized the garden and the orchard that he planted. The fruit and vegetables fed the patients better than they had ever been fed before.

Moreover, the animals made the patients feel at home. What Schweitzer built was not really a hospital; it was a village with medical facilities, where African families were happy to come and to live and look after their sick while they recovered.

To raise money he would make whirlwind tours of Europe, lecturing and playing the organ. His energy was overwhelming.

And though he had originally gone to Africa to lose himself and be forgotten, now his fame grew all the time.

Then came World War II. Another advantage of the simple way the hospital was organized, without elaborate technology, was that when supplies were cut off, the place was self-sufficient.

However, the European doctors and nurses who had joined Schweitzer as volunteers had to go back to their countries, and throughout most of that war Schweitzer, now in his mid-sixties, held the hospital together almost alone. He could take only the most urgent cases.

And then, miraculously, Hélène arrived. Despite her sickness she had managed to find trains and boats that brought her to her husband's side at this time of most need. But the struggle was almost too much. By the time the war ended they were again penniless and worn out. Schweitzer had to think about giving up.

It was the arrival of some American missionaries that saved him. They sent money and supplies, and they publicized his hospital so well that soon it was in every picture magazine in the United States. *Life* magazine called him "the greatest man in the world." He was implored to come to America, and finally gave in.

He was lionized — and he loved it. It meant that Reverence for Life became a household phrase. Schoolchildren all over the world at that time learned to respect life because of Albert Schweitzer. Now we all know about our debt to the environment. Schweitzer was starting from almost nothing. There has probably never been such an influential figure in the fight for the preservation of our planet.

The internal combustion engine came to Lambaréné, and you could get there by air. There were also many new drugs. It became possible to treat leprosy for the first time. Then came penicillin and the other antibiotics. Schweitzer welcomed them all, but warned that indiscriminate use even of these "miracle" drugs would set up a resistance. His lone voice was mocked by some young doctors, but, as ever, he was right.

It was not the only point of argument. The hospital became a place for tourists to visit, and the tourists noticed that the hygiene was not what they were accustomed to in a hospital. They complained that they had been deceived. They never quite understood that the hospital was a village for Africans, not a showplace for wealthy visitors, and Schweitzer was too busy to explain.

Unscrupulous journalists cashed in on the chance to pull down an idol — and suddenly the great dream was in danger. Offers were made to Schweitzer to fund a shining new hospital, all chromium and plate glass and air conditioning. He refused, on behalf of the Africans who liked the place the way it was. Those who wanted a new kind of hospital would have to wait till he died.

The turning point was the Nobel Peace Prize in 1952 and a series of talks he gave over the radio, broadcast worldwide, about the threat of the hydrogen bomb. Again his stock was high and despite a few dissenting voices remained high till his death. The "something small in the spirit of Jesus" was still small in physical scope, but it had spread its seeds throughout the world. And it was still suffused with the spirit of Jesus. When asked why he had gone to Africa, Schweitzer would often reply, "Because my Master sent me."

His daughter, Rhena, who saw little of him as a child, came in her forties to question what he was doing, and stayed to work in the laboratory.

Hélène died first. He lived till his ninetieth year, working harder than most of the young doctors who came to help. At last, one day, he felt very tired. For once he didn't appear at his door at dawn. He managed a last trip round the hospital in an open car and then lay down. A few days later he was dead.

The hospital is still there, now much modernized, and supported both by donations and by the independent Gabonese government. But perhaps Schweitzer's greatest gift is his example of faith and passion combined with common sense — his demonstration that a man can live what he believes — and his saying that anyone can have a Lambaréné, anywhere.

1

Jesus and the Kingdom of God

Everything that Schweitzer thought, did, and said was permeated with his awareness of Jesus, so that it is not always easy to separate his writings on Jesus from those on the many other topics that concerned him.

For example, in his two huge books on the music of J. S. Bach, though they do indeed put forward a completely revolutionary view of Bach as a great painter of emotion, he is constantly aware that all the music is deeply religious in nature. The St. Matthew Passion and the St. John Passion express Bach's faith and his profound understanding of the events and emotions of Christ's death — the cantatas especially. And Schweitzer brings his own profound understanding to the music, an understanding born of his own musicianship and his constant performing of Bach on organ and piano, as well as his focus on Jesus. Again, the whole great enterprise of the hospital he built in the African jungle was driven by his need to diminish suffering in the name of Jesus.

And his own great contribution to philosophy and ethics, Reverence for Life, he described as "the ethic of love widened into universality. It is the ethic of Jesus, now recognized as a logical consequence of thought."

The place, however, where his thoughts about Jesus are most explicit is in his seminal book The Mystery of the Kingdom of

God. *Here we see most clearly his extraordinary combination of deep research, cold, ruthless analysis, and passionate personal dedication.*

For here he lays out his revolutionary thesis that everything that Jesus said and did was driven by the belief that the Kingdom of God was at hand — not just in a spiritual sense but in the very specific sense that the Prophets had foretold, the end of the world as we know it and the coming of the new dispensation in which the lion would lie down with the lamb and the Son of Man, the Messiah, would rule over a world transformed, a place of total peace and harmony. I have quoted a good deal of this book, omitting the section in which Schweitzer summarized and then criticized what he called "the modern-historical solution" to the riddle of the Gospels, which he felt only led to large gaps in our understanding of the process by which Jesus came to his death. Some of this solution is still adhered to by theologians, but the important thing about the book is Schweitzer's solution.

A larger book followed, The Quest of the Historical Jesus, *but this was almost entirely devoted to the attempts of the theologians of the previous century to understand the historical Jesus and Schweitzer's trenchant demonstration of their errors. Reading this, one can understand why fellow scholars regarded him with some alarm as a ruthless but horribly convincing opponent.*

As in everything else, Schweitzer was not prepared to accept the pronouncements of even the highest authority without question. "The judgment of the early church is not binding upon us," he wrote. He felt that huge accretions of meaningless dogma had come between the churches and the Man they celebrated, and that it was time to clear away the rubble and find the treasure buried beneath. He brought to his task a unique combination of meticulous scholarship and deep imaginative insight. Where others felt it sacrilegious to tread — entering into the mind of the founder of his religion and seeking to understand its human reactions as well as its historical context and its conditioning by the beliefs and traditions of its time — Schweitzer unhesitatingly placed his large, confident feet as he sought the truth, not like a normal theologian, but like a detective, assembling the clues that tell him precisely who did what and why. For whatever else Jesus might have been, he was a man and a friend.

So fundamental to Schweitzer's thinking is The Mystery of the Kingdom of God, *and so closely argued, that to cut or condense is very hard and sure to be misleading. Reading this book one might initially feel that he is cold and super-analytical. And then one reads the Postscript and realizes that under the skin of the German academic is a heart of sensitivity and passion — a passion not only for the immense, heroic figure he studies, but also for truth; and that the truth saves him from any self-indulgent sentimentality.*

Essential to the understanding of Schweitzer's thought is the word "eschatology." Eschatology means the study of the last things. In this context the last things are obviously the end of history and the coming of the new dispensation. This was what the Jews had been promised and what they were waiting for. And this is what Jesus believed he would bring about by his crucifixion. He would return as the Messiah.

It failed to happen. And so when after many years of waiting, the disciples, now under much pressure to explain what went wrong, started to write down what they remembered of their lives with Jesus, the eschatology was not there because he had never really told them about it. His coming messiahship had to be kept secret, and they would know about it when it happened. So they were able to remember only historically. And all theologians ever since have been forced to see and explain the life and motives of Jesus in historical terms and have therefore failed to understand them.

To those who might feel that we are dealing with long-dead and irrelevant issues, I would point out that if one were to

*take Schweitzer's conclusions seriously, it would instantly de-
molish the basis of the fundamentalist Christianity that is rife at
present, and indeed of very many branches of the church.*

*Schweitzer recognized that, however convincing his argu-
ments, they had failed to be accepted by the churches and by
individual Christians, and he attributed this, surely rightly, to
the difficulties that they raise for the traditional Christian faith.
But he was also right to note that Christianity would do well
to pay attention to the truth, rather than to deep-rooted traditional error. The constant leaking away of thoughtful people
from the churches may well be the penalty the churches pay for
this intransigence.*

*But what is perhaps the most astonishing and impressive ev-
idence of Schweitzer's ruthless honesty lies in the conclusion to*
The Quest. *Here he dismisses all his high scholarship, all his
unending research and the midnight oil that he has burnt in
writing his two great books, and says that the historical Jesus
hardly matters. Truth matters, yes, but what really matters is
knowing Jesus in the Spirit, which is above history.*

JESUS

True Historians

*Schweitzer wrote the following about another man, Reimarus,
the earliest biblical critic, but it could well be applied to him.*

The fact is there are some who are historians by the grace of
God, who from their mother's womb have an instinctive feeling
for the real. They follow through all the intricacy and confusion
of reported fact the pathway of reality, like a stream which, despite the rocks that encumber its course and the windings of
its valley, finds its way inevitably to the sea. No erudition can

supply the place of this historical instinct, but erudition sometimes serves a useful purpose, inasmuch as it produces in its
possessors the pleasing belief that they are historians, and thus
secures their services for the cause of history. In truth, they are
at best merely doing the preliminary spadework of history, collecting for a future historian the dry bones of fact, from which,
with the aid of his natural gift, he can recall the past to life.
More often, however, the way in which erudition seeks to serve
history is by suppressing historical discoveries as long as possible and leading an army of possibilities out into the field to
oppose the one true view. By arraying these in support of one
another it finally imagines that it has created out of possibilities
a living reality.

   This obstructive erudition is the special prerogative of theology, in which, even at the present day, a truly marvelous
scholarship often serves only to blind the eyes to elementary
truths and to cause the artificial to be preferred to the natural.

— The Quest of the Historical Jesus

The Mystery of the Kingdom of God *(extracts)*

The attempt to write a life of Jesus, beginning not at the beginning but in the middle, with the thought of the Passion, must
surely be made sometime. Strange that it has not been made
before, for it is in the air!

   The fact is that all presentations of the life of Jesus are sat-
isfactory up to a certain point: the inception of the thought of
the Passion. There, however, the connection fails. Not one of
them succeeds in explaining why Jesus now suddenly finds that
his death is necessary, and in what sense he sees it as a saving
act. To establish this connection one must try the experiment of
making the thought of the Passion the point of departure, so as
to make sense of the earlier and later periods of the life of Jesus.
If we fail to understand the idea of the Passion, perhaps that is
because we have formed a mistaken notion of the first period

of his life and thus automatically made it impossible to see how the Passion idea was born.

Recent years of research have revealed on what slight grounds our historical conception of the life of Jesus really rests. We have to admit that we are faced with a difficult dilemma. Either Jesus really took himself to be the Messiah, or (as a new trend of thought now seems to suggest) this dignity was first ascribed to him by the early church. In either case the Life of Jesus remains equally puzzling. If Jesus really regarded himself as the Messiah, how is it that he acted as if he were not the Messiah? How can we explain the way that his office and dignity seem to have nothing to do with his public activity? How can we account for the fact that only after his public activity was ended (excluding the last few days at Jerusalem) did he disclose to his disciples who he was, at the same time forbidding them ever to speak of this secret? It explains nothing to suggest that his motives were due to prudence or the wish to instruct. In the Synoptical accounts where is there even the slightest hint that Jesus wished to educate the disciples and the people about his messiahship?

The more one thinks about it the more clearly one sees how little the assumption that Jesus took himself to be the Messiah explains his "life": there is no connection whatever between his self-awareness and his public activity. It may sound banal to ask the question, but it cannot be avoided: Why did Jesus never try to teach the people the new ethical conception of messiahship? The attempt would not have been so hopeless as is often as-sumed, for at that time there was a deep spiritual movement going on in Israel. Why did Jesus maintain persistent silence about his conception of messiahship?

On the other hand, if we assume that he did *not* take him-self to be the Messiah, we must explain how he came to be made the Messiah after his death. Certainly it was not on the ground of his public activity, for this had nothing to do with his messiahship. But then again, what was the significance of the revelation of the secret of his messiahship to the Twelve and the confession before the high priest? It is a mere act of violence to declare these scenes unhistorical. If one embarks on this kind of ruthlessness, what is there left of the whole gospel tradition?

At the same time one should not forget that if Jesus did not take himself to be the Messiah, this means the death blow to the Christian faith. The judgment of the early church is not binding upon us. The Christian religion is founded upon the messianic consciousness of Jesus, through which he himself made a sharp distinction between himself and the ranks of other preachers of religious morality. If he did not take himself to be the Messiah, then the whole of Christianity rests — to use honestly a much perverted and abused word — upon a "value judgment" formed by the adherents of Jesus of Nazareth after his death!

Only one conclusion can be drawn from this dilemma, namely, that what has hitherto been accepted as the "historical" conception of the messianic consciousness of Jesus is false — because it does not explain the history. The only truly historical conception is one that explains how Jesus could take himself to be the Messiah without feeling obliged to make this consciousness affect his public ministry for the Kingdom of God — rather, how indeed he was compelled to make his messianic status a secret! Why did the messiahship of Jesus remain his secret? To explain this means to understand his life. . . .

The early Christian faith had not the least interest in this earthly life, because the messiahship of Jesus was grounded upon his resurrection, not upon his earthly ministry, and the disciples, looking forward expectantly to the coming of the Messiah in glory, were interested in the earthly life of Jesus of Nazareth only insofar as it served to illustrate his sayings. There was absolutely no such thing as an early Christian conception of the life of Jesus, and the Synoptic Gospels contain nothing of the sort. They string together the narratives of the events of his public ministry without trying to make their sequence and connection intelligible, or to enable us to observe the "development" of Jesus. Then, in the course of time, as the eschatological expectation waned, as the emphasis on the earthly appearance of Jesus as the Messiah began to dominate, so leading to a particular view (a theory) of the life of Jesus, the accounts of his public ministry had already assumed so fixed a form that they could not be altered by this process.

•

The "Life of Jesus" is limited to the last months of his existence on earth. He began his ministry at the season of the summer seed-sowing and ended it on the cross at Easter of the following year.

His public ministry may be counted in weeks. The first period extends from seed time to harvest; the second comprises the days of his appearance in Jerusalem. Autumn and winter he spent in heathen territory alone with his disciples.

Before him the Baptist had appeared and had borne emphatic witness to the nearness of the Kingdom and the coming of the mighty pre-messianic Forerunner, with whose appearance the pouring out of the Holy Ghost should take place. According to Joel, this among other miracles was the sign that the Day of Judgment was imminent. John himself never imagined that he was this Forerunner; nor did such a thought occur to the people, for he had not ushered in the age of miracles. He was a prophet — that was the universal opinion.

About Jesus' earlier development we know nothing. All lies in the dark. Only this is sure: at his baptism the secret of his existence was disclosed to him — namely, that he was the one whom God had destined to be the Messiah. With this revelation he was complete and underwent no further development. For now he is assured that, until the near coming of the messianic age which was to reveal his glorious dignity, he has to labor for the Kingdom as the unrecognized and hidden Messiah and must approve and purify himself together with his friends in the final Affliction.

The idea of suffering was thus included in his messianic consciousness, just as the notion of the pre-messianic Affliction was indissolubly connected with the expectation of the Kingdom. Earthly events could not influence Jesus' course. His secret raised him above the world, even though he still walked as a man among men.

His appearing and his proclamation have to do only with the imminence of the Kingdom. His preaching is that of John, only that he confirms it by signs. Although his secret controls all his preaching, yet no one may know of it, for he must remain unrecognized till the new eon dawns.

His whole ethical outlook, like his secret, is ruled by the contrast of "Now and Then." It is a question of repentance that prepares people for the Kingdom, and the achievement of the righteousness that makes them fit for it — for only the righteous inherit the Kingdom. This righteousness is higher than that of the Law; for Jesus knows that the law and the Prophets were sufficient until John, but with the Baptist one finds oneself in the age of the Forerunner, immediately before the dawn of the Kingdom.

Therefore, as the future Messiah, he must preach and work that higher morality. The poor in spirit, the meek, those that endure suffering, those that hunger and thirst after righteousness, the merciful, the pure in heart, the peacemakers — these all are blessed because these qualities destine them for the Kingdom.

Behind this ethical preaching looms the secret of the Kingdom of God.... As the plentiful harvest, by God's wonderful working, follows mysteriously upon the sowing, so also the Kingdom of God arrives by reason of man's moral renewal, but substantially without his assistance.

The parable contains also the suggestion of a chronological coincidence. Jesus spoke at the season of seed-sowing and expected the Kingdom at the time of the harvest. Nature was God's clock. With the last seed-sowing he had set it for the last time.

The secret of the Kingdom of God is the celestial transfigura-
tion of the ethics of the early prophets, according to which also
the final state of glory will be brought about by God only on
condition of the moral conversion of Israel. In masterful style
Jesus effects the synthesis of the apocalyptic of Daniel and the
ethics of the Prophets....

A third element in the preaching of the Kingdom was the
intimation of the pre-messianic Affliction. Believers must be prepared to pass with him through that time of trial, in which they
are to prove themselves the elect of the Kingdom by steadfast
resistance to the last attack of the power of the world. This
attack will concentrate about his person; therefore they must
stand by him even unto death. Only life in God's Kingdom is
real life. The Son of Man will judge them according as they
have stood by him, Jesus, or not. Thus Jesus at the conclusion
of the Beatitudes turns to his own disciples with the words:
"Blessed are ye when men persecute you for my sake." The
charge to the Apostles turns into a consideration of the Affliction. The message to the Baptist about the imminence of the
Kingdom concludes with the words: "Blessed is he whosoever
shall not be offended in me." At Bethsaida, the morning after
he had celebrated the supper by the seashore, he adjured the
multitude to stand by him, even when he would become an object of shame and scorn in this sinful world. Their blessedness
depends upon this.

This Affliction means not only a probation but also an atonement. It is foreordained in the messianic drama, because God
requires of the adherents of the Kingdom a satisfaction for their
transgressions in this age. But he is almighty. In this omnipotence he determines the question of membership in the Kingdom
and the place each shall occupy, without himself being bound by
any determining cause whatsoever. So also in view of his omnipotence the necessity of the final Affliction is only relative. He
can set it aside. The last three petitions of the Lord's Prayer consider this possibility. After praying to God that he will send the

Kingdom, that his name may be blessed, and his will be done on earth as it is in heaven, men beg him to forgive them their transgressions and spare them the Temptation, rescuing them directly from the power of evil.

This was the content of Jesus' preaching during the first period. Throughout this time he remained on the northern shore of the lake. Chorazin, Bethsaida, and Capernaum were the principal centers of his activity. From there he made an excursion across the lake to the region of the Ten Cities and a journey to Nazareth.

It was precisely in the towns where he was most active that he encountered unbelief. The curse that he was forced to utter over them is proof of it. The Pharisees, moreover, were hostile and sought to discredit him with the people on account of his very miracles. In Nazareth he had experience of the fact that a prophet is without honor in his own country.

Thus the Galilean period was anything but a fortunate one. Such outward ill success, however, signified nothing for the coming of the Kingdom. The unbelieving cities merely brought down judgment upon themselves. Jesus had other mysterious indications for measuring the approach of the Kingdom. By these he recognized that the time was come, and that was why he sent out the Apostles just as they were returning from Nazareth; for it was harvest time.

By means of their preaching and their signs the reputation of his mighty personality spread far and wide. Now begins the time of success! John in prison hears of it and sends his disciples to ask him if he is "he that should come," since from his miracles he concluded that the time of the mighty Forerunner whom he had heralded had arrived.

He had heard that Jesus performed signs, that his disciples had power over the spirits; that when he spoke of the Judgment he laid stress on the fact that the Son of Man stood in such solidarity with him that he would recognize only those who had stood by him, Jesus. The people therefore were thinking that he might be the one for whom all were looking, and the Baptist desired to have assurance on this point.

Jesus cannot tell him who he is. "The time is far advanced" — that is the gist of his reply. After the departure of the messengers Jesus turns to the people and signifies in mysterious terms that the time is indeed much further advanced than the Baptist dreamed in asking such a question. The era of the Forerunner had already begun with the appearance of the Baptist himself. From that time on the Kingdom of God is compelled to draw near.

The sending out of the Twelve was the last effort to bring about the Kingdom. When they returned and told him of their success and reported that they had power over the evil spirits, it showed to him that all was ready, and he expected the immediate dawn of the Kingdom. He had even doubted whether the Twelve would return before it happened and had said to them that the appearing of the Son of Man could overtake them before they had gone through all the cities of Israel.

His work is done. Now he needs to collect himself and to be alone with his disciples. They take a boat and sail along the coast towards the north. But the crowd that had gathered around him at the preaching of the disciples now want to await the Kingdom with him. They follow along the shore and surprise Jesus and the disciples when they land on a lonely beach.

As it was evening the disciples want him to send the people away to find food in the neighboring hamlets. For him, however, the hour is too solemn to be profaned by an earthly meal. Before sending them away he tells them to sit down, and he celebrates with them an anticipation of the messianic feast. To the community gathered around him to await the Kingdom, he, the Messiah to be, distributes hallowed food, thus mysteriously consecrating them to be partakers of the heavenly banquet. Because they do not know his secret, neither they nor the disciples understand the significance of his act. They only know that it means something wonderfully solemn, and they question about it among themselves.

Then he sends them away. He orders the disciples to skirt the coast to Bethsaida. For his part he goes up into the mountain to pray and then follows along the shore on foot. Seeing his figure in the darkness of the night, and still under the spell of the supper where he stood before them in mysterious majesty — they believe that this is a supernatural apparition that approaches them over the turbulent waves through which they are toiling to the shore. The morning after the supper by the seashore he collects the people and the disciples at Bethsaida and warns them to stand by him and not to deny him in the coming humiliation.

Six days later he goes with the Three to the mountain where he had prayed alone. There he is revealed to them as the Messiah. On the way home he forbids them to speak about it until he is revealed at the Resurrection in the glory of the Son of Man. They, however, still remark on the failure of Elijah to appear, who must come before the Resurrection of the dead can take place. So he must now make it clear to them that the beheaded prisoner John the Baptist was Elijah. They should take no offense at his fate, for it was so ordained. He who is to be Son of Man must also suffer many things and be set at naught. The Scripture says so.

But the Kingdom that Jesus expected so soon failed to appear. This first eschatological delay and postponement was momentous for the fate of the gospel tradition: all the events related to the mission of the Twelve now became unintelligible, because nobody was aware of the intense eschatological expectation that at that time inspired Jesus and his following. This is why this period is confused and obscure in the accepted accounts of it, and all the more so because several incidents remained mysterious even to those who took part in them. Thus the sacramental supper by the seashore became in the tradition a "miraculous feeding" in a sense totally different from that which Jesus had in mind.

Similarly, the motives of Jesus' disappearance became unintelligible. It seems to be a case of flight, though the accounts give no hint as to how this could have come about.

The key to the historical understanding of the life of Jesus lies
in the recognition of the two moments in which the eschatological expectation culminated. During the days at Jerusalem there
was a return of the enthusiasm which the people had already
shown at Bethsaida. Without this assumption we are left with
a yawning gap in the gospel tradition between the mission of
the Twelve and the journey to Jerusalem. Historians find themselves compelled to invent a period of Galilean defeat in order
to establish some connection between the recorded facts — as if
a section were missing in our Gospels. *That is the weak point
of all the "lives of Jesus."*

By retreating into the region of the Genesareth Jesus with-
drew from the Pharisees and the people in order to be alone
with his disciples, as he had in vain tried to do since their return from their mission. He urgently needed such a retreat,
for he had to come to an understanding about two messianic
questions:

Why is the Baptist executed by the secular authority before
the messianic time has dawned?

Why does the Kingdom fail to appear even though the tokens
of its dawning are present?

The secret is made known to him through the Scripture: God
brings the Kingdom about *without the general Affliction.* He
whom God has destined to reign in glory accomplishes it himself by being tried as a malefactor and condemned, allowing the
others to go free: He makes the atonement for them. What does
it matter if they believe that God is punishing him, or if this di-
minishes him in their eyes after he has preached righteousness
to them? After his Passion the glory will dawn, and then they
will see that it was for them that he suffered.

This was the destiny allotted to him by God that Jesus read
in the Prophet Isaiah: he was the Chosen One. The death of the
Baptist showed him the manner in which he was to suffer this
condemnation: he must be put to death by the secular authority
as a malefactor in the sight of all the people. He must therefore

make his way up to Jerusalem for the season when all Israel is gathered there.

So as soon as the time comes for the Passover pilgrimage he sets out with his disciples. Before they leave the north country, he asks them who the people take him to be. They can only reply that he is seen as Elijah. But Peter, mindful of the revelation on the mountain near Bethsaida, says: Thou art the Son of God. And then Jesus informs them of his secret. Yes, it is he who will be revealed as Son of Man at the Resurrection. But before that, it is decreed that he must be delivered to the high priests and elders to be condemned and put to death. God so wills it. This is the reason why they are going up to Jerusalem.

Peter resents this new disclosure, for nothing of this kind was said in the revelation on the mountain. He takes Jesus apart and appeals to him energetically. But he is sharply rebuked for listening to human considerations when God speaks.

This journey to Jerusalem is the funeral march to victory. Within the secret of the Passion lies concealed the secret of the Kingdom. They march after him, knowing only that when all this is accomplished he will be the Messiah. They are sorrowful for what must come to pass; they do not understand why it must be so, and they dare not ask him. But above all, their thoughts are occupied about the conditions that await them in the approaching Kingdom. When he is the Messiah, what will they be? That occupies their minds, and they talk about it among themselves. But he rebukes them and explains why he must suffer: only through humiliation and by meekly sacrificing oneself in the service of others is one made fit to reign in the Kingdom of God. So he, who will exercise supreme authority as Son of Man, must now make atonement for many by meekly sacrificing his life for them.

The second period of Jesus' public ministry begins with their arrival in Jewish territory. He is again surrounded by the people. In Jericho a crowd gathers to see him pass through. The healing of a blind beggar, the son of Timaeus, convinces people

that he is the great Forerunner, just as they thought already
in Galilee. The jubilant multitudes prepare for him a festal
entry into Jerusalem. They acclaim him with Hosanna as the
one who according to prophecy precedes the Messiah. Hosanna
in the highest, however, is their acclaim of the Kingdom that
is about to appear. The same situation is reached again as in
the great days near Bethsaida: Jesus is thronged by the multitudes expectant of the Kingdom. The message of the parables
spoken in Jerusalem has to do with the nearness of the Kingdom. The parables are warnings, with a note of menace as
well for those that harden their hearts against the message.
The question, however, that agitates men's minds is not, Is he
the Messiah, or not? but, Is the Kingdom as near as he says,
or not?

The Pharisees and scribes have no idea that the hour has
struck. They show a complete lack of awareness of the nearness
of the Kingdom; otherwise they could not have put to him questions that at this advanced hour have lost all significance. What
difference does it make now about the Roman tribute? What
do the far-fetched Sadduceean arguments amount to against the
imminence of the resurrection of the dead? Soon, with the advent of the Kingdom, all earthly rule is done away, as well as
earthly human nature itself.

If only they understood the signs of the times! He puts to
them two questions, which should make them ponder and become aware that the time they live in is pregnant with a great
secret that is not dreamed of in the learning of the scribes.

By what authority did the Baptist act? If they knew that he
was the Forerunner, as Jesus had mysteriously suggested to the
people, then they must know too that the hour of the Kingdom
had struck.

*How is the Messiah at one time David's Son — that is, subor-
dinate to him; at another, David's Lord — that is, his superior?*
If they could explain that, they would also understand how he

who works for God's Kingdom, now lowly and unknown, will be revealed as Lord and Christ.

But as it is they do not even suspect that the messianic indications harbor secrets. With all their learning they are blind leaders of the blind, who, instead of making the people receptive for the Kingdom, harden their hearts, and instead of drawing out from the Law the higher morality which renders men fit for the Kingdom, work against it with their petty outward precepts and draw the people after them to perdition. Hence: Woe to the Pharisees and scribes!

True, even among them are some that have kept their eyes open. The scribe who put to him the question about the great commandment and welcomed his reply is commended as "having understanding" and therefore "not far from the Kingdom of God"; he will belong to it when it appears.

The mass of the Pharisees and scribes, however, understand him so little that they decree his death. But they have no effective charge to bring against his behavior: a disrespectful word about the Temple — that is all.

Then Judas betrays the secret to them. Now he is condemned.

As death nears, Jesus draws himself up to the same triumphant stature as in the days by the seaside — for with death comes the Kingdom. As on that occasion he celebrated with the believers a mystic feast as an anticipation of the messianic banquet, so now he rises at the end of the last earthly supper and distributes to the disciples hallowed food and drink, intimating to them with a solemn voice that this is their last earthly meal, for they are soon to be united at the banquet in the Father's Kingdom. A twofold parable suggests the secret of the Passion. For him, the bread and wine that he hands them at the supper are his body and his blood, for by sacrificing himself to death he ushers in the messianic feast. But the parable remains obscure to the disciples. Indeed, its purpose was not to explain anything to them — *for it was an enigma-parable.*

Now, as the great hour approaches, just as after the supper by the seashore, he again seeks a lonely spot where he may pray. He bears the Affliction for others. Therefore he can say to the disciples beforehand that in the night they will all be offended in him — and he does not need to condemn them, for this is what the Scripture has determined. What endless peace lies in these words! Indeed, he comforts them: after the Resurrection he will gather them about him and go before them into Galilee in messianic glory, retracing the same road along which they had followed him on his way to death.

It still remains, however, within the scope of God's omnipotence to eliminate the Affliction for him also. So, just as once he prayed with the believers, "And lead us not into the Temptation," so now he prays for himself that God may save his lips from the cup of suffering. But if it is God's will, he feels strong enough to drink it. He is sorrowful rather for the Three. The sons of Zebedee, to gain the seats upon the throne, have boasted that they can drink with him the cup of suffering and receive with him the baptism of suffering. Peter swore that he would stand by him even if he must die with him. He does not know what God has ordained for them — whether he will lay upon them what they desire to undertake. Therefore he tells them to stay near him. And while he prays to God for himself, he thinks of them and twice wakes them up, telling them to stay awake and beseech God not to lead them through the Temptation.

The third time he comes to them the betrayer with his band is near. The hour has come. He draws himself up to the full stature of his majesty. He is alone; his disciples flee.

The hearing of witnesses is merely a pretence. After they have gone the high priest puts directly the question about the messiahship. "I am," says Jesus, referring them at the same time to the hour when he will appear as Son of Man on the clouds of heaven surrounded by the angels. Therefore he is found guilty of blasphemy and condemned to death.

On the afternoon of the fourteenth of Nisan, as the Paschal lamb is eaten in the evening, he gives a loud cry and dies.

•

The judgments passed upon this realistic account of the life of Jesus may be very diverse, according to the dogmatic, historical, or literary points of view of the critics. But with the *aim* of the book they may not find fault: *to depict the figure of Jesus in its overwhelming heroic greatness and to impress it on the modern age and on modern theology.*

The heroic is fading from our modern *Weltanschauung,* our Christianity, and our conception of the person of Jesus. For this reason men have humanized and humbled him. Renan has stripped off his halo and reduced him to a sentimental figure, coward spirits like Schopenhauer have dared to appeal to him for their enervating philosophy, and our generation has modernized him, with the notion that it could comprehend his character and development psychologically.

We must go back to the point where we can feel again the heroic in Jesus. Before that mysterious Person, who, in the manner of his time, knew that he was creating on the foundation of his life and death a moral world that bears his name, we must be forced to lay our faces in the dust, without daring even to wish to understand his nature. Only then can the heroic in our Christianity and in our *Weltanschauung* come back to life.

— *The Mystery of the Kingdom of God*

Letter (undated) to Hélène Bresslau, Later to Be His Wife, Referring to The Mystery of the Kingdom of God

Would you like to participate in the joy I feel at the completion of this final chapter? Remain for me what you are — in order to find the right path, one has to be guided, encouraged, also admired and scolded.

The Quest of the Historical Jesus *(extracts)*

The history of the critical study of the life of Jesus is of higher intrinsic value than the history of the study of ancient dogma or of the attempts to create a new one. It has to describe the most tremendous thing which the religious consciousness has ever dared and done....

[It concerns] the most vital thing in the world's history. There came a Man to rule over the world; He ruled it for good and for ill, as history testifies; He destroyed the world into which He was born; the spiritual life of our own time seems likely to perish at His hands, for He leads to battle against our thought a host of dead ideas, a ghostly army upon which death has no power, and Himself destroys again the truth and goodness which His Spirit creates in us, so that it cannot rule the world. That He continues, notwithstanding, to reign as the alone Great and alone True in a world of which He denied the continuance is the prime example of that antithesis between spiritual and natural truth which underlies all life and all events, and in Him emerges into the field of history.

•

The study of the Life of Jesus has had a curious history. It set out in quest of the historical Jesus, believing that when it had found Him it could bring Him straight into our time as a Teacher and Savior. It loosed the bands by which He had been riveted for centuries to the stony rocks of ecclesiastical doctrine and rejoiced to see life and movement coming into the figure once more, and the historical Jesus advancing, as it seemed, to meet it. But He does not stay; He passes by our time and re-turns to His own. What surprised and dismayed the theology of the last forty years was that, despite all forced and arbitrary interpretations, it could not keep Him in our time, but had to let Him go. He returned to His own time, not owing to the ap-plication of any historical ingenuity, but by the same inevitable necessity by which the liberated pendulum returns to its original position....

Jesus means something to our world because a mighty spiritual force streams forth from Him and flows through our time also. This fact can neither be shaken nor confirmed by any historical discovery. It is the solid foundation of Christianity....

We are experiencing what Paul experienced. In the very moment when we were coming nearer to the historical Jesus than men had ever come before, and were already stretching out our hands to draw Him into our own time, we have been obliged to give up the attempt and acknowledge our failure in that paradoxical saying: "If we have known Christ after the flesh yet henceforth know we Him no more." And further we must be prepared to find that the historical knowledge of the personality and life of Jesus will not be a help, but perhaps even an offense to religion. But the truth is, it is not Jesus as historically known, but Jesus as spiritually arisen within men, who is significant for our time and can help it. Not the historical Jesus, but the spirit which goes forth from Him and in the spirits of men strives for new influence and rule is that which overcomes the world....

For that reason it is a good thing that the true historical Jesus should overthrow the modern Jesus, should rise up against the modern spirit and send upon earth, not peace, but a sword. He was not a teacher, not a casuist; He was an imperious ruler. It was because He was so in His inmost being that He could think of Himself as the Son of Man. That was only the temporally conditioned expression of the fact that He was an authoritative ruler. The names in which men expressed their recognition of Him as such, Messiah, Son of Man, Son of God, have become for us historical parables. We can find no designation that expresses what He is for us.

He comes to us as One unknown, without a name, as of old, by the lakeside, He came to those men who knew Him not. He speaks to us the same word, "Follow thou me," and sets us to the tasks that He has to fulfil for our time. He commands. And to those who obey Him, whether they be wise or simple, He will reveal Himself in the toils, the conflicts, the sufferings which they shall pass through in His fellowship, and, as an ineffable mystery, they shall learn in their own experience Who He is.

— The Quest of the Historical Jesus

Introduction to the Third Edition (1950) of The Quest of the Historical Jesus

The fundamental problem which stands out more and more clearly is whether Jesus builds on the presuppositions of later Jewish eschatology concerning the coming of the Kingdom of God and the Messiah, or upon a non-eschatological foundation. This question was argued in lives of Jesus for three and a half generations....

The latest literature on the subject does not seem to me likely to lead to any new presentation of the problem comparable with that which led to the earlier challenge to decide for or against the claim that the thought of Jesus was eschatological in character. A decision so momentous is no longer possible.

The decision in favor of eschatology is hardly likely to be questioned again. It provides the only trustworthy clue to the text of Matthew and Mark, allowing words to remain as they stand, with their ordinary meaning. Otherwise, meanings have to be read into the text, and the sincere student must entertain far-reaching doubts as to its trustworthiness.

The fact remains, however, that the eschatological solution has not succeeded in dominating the latest writing on the life of Jesus, and is not within sight of doing so. It is in the remarkable position of not being disproved and, at the same time, not being fully accepted. The reason for the latter is that its historical value is overshadowed by the difficulties which it raises for the traditional Christian faith.

It is an axiom for tradition that Jesus preached truth utterly beyond and above the time-process. But this is contradicted by the eschatological picture of Jesus, which shows him sharing the expectations of his contemporaries. Faith is asked to give up something which it has always held and cannot contemplate abandoning. We may therefore expect lives of Jesus to go on being written that try to avoid the challenge which has launched scientific research on a course from which it cannot turn back. These will make far-reaching concessions, as indeed they must, but all the same they will continue to believe that somehow Jesus thought in a way that was not eschatological. Their aim is to pay due respect to history and at the same time give as little offense as possible to faith. The old procedure is glossed over and made acceptable by the adoption of modern methods.

The latest excursions in this direction are of less interest and importance. The supreme question for today and tomorrow is how to explain the relation of Christian faith with historical truth, and how to state the result of that relation. It follows from historical study of Jesus, early Christianity, and the growth of dogma that Christians are faced with the difficult task of giving an account of the growth of their religion, and of maintaining that its present form is due to its development. No other religion has had to meet such a demand, or would have been equal to it.

The present situation compels faith to distinguish between the essence and the form of religious truth. The ideas through which it finds expression may change as time goes on, without destroying its essence. Its brightness is not dimmed by what happens to it. Changing seems to make the ideas more transparent as means whereby the truth is revealed.

Historical research not only compels us to recognize change; it also shows us what is actually happening, viz., that the type of idea employed for the expression of religious truth becomes increasingly spiritual.

The gospel of the Kingdom of God came into the world in its late-Jewish form, which it could not retain. The Kingdom, expected to come immediately in supernatural fashion, fails to appear, and so does the Son of Man, who was to arrive on the clouds of heaven. The situation thus created compelled believers to take a more and more spiritual view of the Kingdom of God and the messiahship of Jesus, the former becoming a spiritual and ethical ideal to be realized in this world, and Jesus the spiritual Messiah who laid its foundation through his ethical teaching. So obvious did this appear that it was taken to be the view of Jesus himself, and his preaching was understood in this sense. All this involves overlooking the words of the first two Gospels, which create a different impression.

Respect for historical truth, however, compels our faith to give up this naivete and to admit that it has been subject to development. It can do this without being untrue to itself or to Jesus. It has become what it is under the pressure of a higher necessity, under the influence of the Spirit of Jesus.

It was Jesus who began to spiritualize the ideas of the Kingdom of God and the Messiah. He introduced into the late-Jewish conception of the Kingdom his strong ethical emphasis on love, making this and the consistent practice of it the indispensable condition of entrance. By so doing he charged the late-Jewish idea of the Kingdom of God with ethical forces, which transformed it into the spiritual and ethical reality with which we are familiar. Since the faith clung firmly to the ethical note, so dominant in the teaching of Jesus, it was able to reconcile and identify the two, neglecting those utterances in which Jesus voices the older eschatology.

Jesus is already the spiritual Messiah, as opposed to the Messiah of late-Jewish eschatology, in that he has the Messianic consciousness while living a human life in this world and feels himself called to awaken in men the desire for the spiritual qualification for entrance into the Kingdom. Late-Jewish eschatology sees the Messiah only as the supernatural Lord of the supernatural Kingdom of God. It has no idea of his first appearing on earth as a Servant in human form. This came to birth in the consciousness of Jesus. As the spiritual Lord of the spiritual

Kingdom of God on earth, he is the Lord who will rule in our hearts.

It may come as a stumbling block to our faith to find that it was not Jesus himself who gave its perfect spiritual form to the truth which he brought into the world, but that it received this in the course of time through the working of his Spirit. But this is something which we have to overcome. Such is our destiny. The old word still stands. "My thoughts are not your thoughts, neither are your ways my ways, saith the Lord. For as the heavens are higher than the earth, so are my ways higher than your ways, and my thoughts higher than your thoughts" (Isaiah 55:8–9).

Historical truth not only creates difficulties for faith; it also enriches it, by compelling it to examine the importance of the work of the Spirit of Jesus for its growth and continuance. The Gospel cannot simply be taken over; it must be appropriated in his Spirit. What the Bible really offers us is his Spirit, as we find it in him, and in those who first came under its power. Every conviction of faith must be tested by him. Truth in the highest sense is that which is in the Spirit of Jesus.

The faith of the Protestant church is not in the church, but in Christ. That lays upon it the necessity of being truthful in all things. If it gives up the fearless pursuit of truth, it becomes but a shadow of itself — useless to Christianity and to the world.

Research into the life of Jesus proves the honesty of Protestant Christendom. My presentation of its course makes an epoch of scientific Protestant theology live again for future generations. May these share with their predecessors the determination to be truthful, and thereby be assured that unflinching truthfulness is an essential part of real religion.

We may take for our comfort, whenever historical science raises difficulties for faith, Paul's words: "We can do nothing against the truth, but for the truth" (2 Corinthians 13:8).

— *The Quest of the Historical Jesus*

The Existence of Jesus

In the autumn of 1912, when I was already busy shopping and packing, I started working into *The Quest of the Historical Jesus* the new books which had appeared on that subject since its publication, and recasting sections of the work which no longer satisfied me. I was especially concerned to set forth late-Jewish eschatology more thoroughly and better than I had been able to do before because I had ever since been constantly occupied with the subject, and besides that to analyze and discuss the works of John M. Robertson, William Benjamin Smith, James George Frazer, Arthur Drews and others, who contested the historical existence of Jesus. Unfortunately the later English editions of my history are all based on the text of the first German one.

It is no hard matter to assert that Jesus never lived. The attempt to prove it, however, infallibly works round to produce the opposite conclusion.

In Jewish literature of the first century the existence of Jesus is not satisfactorily attested, and in Greek and Latin literature of the same period there is no evidence for it at all. Of the two passages in which the Jewish writer Josephus makes incidental mention of Jesus in his *Antiquities* one was undoubtedly interpolated by Christian copyists. The first pagan witness for His existence is Tacitus, who in the reign of Trajan, in the second decade of the second century A.D., reports in his *Annals* (XV, 44) that the founder of the sect of "Christians," which was accused by Nero of causing the great fire of Rome, was executed under the government of Tiberius by the procurator of Judaea, Pontius Pilate. Anyone, therefore, who is dissatisfied, since Roman history only takes notice of the existence of Jesus because of the continuance of a Christian movement, and that, too, for the first time some eighty years after His death, and who is, further, bent on declaring the Gospels and St. Paul's Epistles to be not genuine, can consider himself justified in refusing to recognize the historical existence of Jesus.

But that does not settle the matter. It still has to be explained when, where, and how Christianity came into existence without either Jesus or Paul; how it came, later on, to wish to trace its origins back to these invented historical personalities; and, finally, for what reasons it took the remarkable course of making these two founders members of the Jewish people. The Gospels and the Epistles of St. Paul can, indeed, be demonstrated to be not genuine only when it is made intelligible how they could have come into existence if they really were not genuine. Of the difficulties of this task which has come to them the champions of the unhistorical character of Jesus take no account, and it is in an inconceivably frivolous way that they go to work. Though they differ from each other widely as to details, the method which they all apply attempts to reach a proof that there existed already in pre-Christian times, in Palestine or elsewhere in the East, a Christ-cult or Jesus-cult of a Gnostic character, the center of which, as in the cults of Anonis, Osiris, and Tammuz, is a god or demi-god who dies and rises again. Since we have no information about any such pre-Christian Christ-cult, its existence must be made as probable as possible by a process of combination and fantasy. Thereon must follow a further act of imagination to the effect that the adherents of this assumed pre-Christian Christ-cult found at some time or other reasons for changing the object of their worship, the god who dies and rises again, into a historic human personality, and, in defiance of the facts known to the various circles of his believers, declaring his cult to have existed only from the date of this change of personality, whereas the other mystery religions show no tendency whatever to recast myths as history. As if this were not difficulty enough, the Gospels and the Pauline Epistles require from these champions of the unhistorical character of Jesus a further explanation of how their Christ-cult, instead of claiming to have originated in a long-past age of no longer verifiable events, lapsed into the mistake of dating its invented Jesus scarcely two or three generations back, and of allowing Him, moreover, to appear on the stage of history as a Jew among Jews.

As the last and hardest task of all comes that of explaining the contents of the Gospels, in detail, as myth changed to history. If they keep to their theory, Drews, Smith, and Robertson must actually maintain that the events and the discourses reported by Matthew and Mark are only the clothing of thoughts which that earlier mystery-religion put forward. The fact that Arthur Drews and others try to establish this explanation by pressing into their service not only every myth they can discover but astronomy and astrology as well, shows what demands it makes upon the imagination.

It is clear, then, as a matter of fact, from the writings of those who dispute the historicity of Jesus that the hypothesis of His existence is a thousand times easier to prove than that of His non-existence. That does not mean that the hopeless undertaking is being abandoned. Again and again books appear about the non-existence of Jesus and find credulous readers, although they contain nothing new or going beyond Robertson, Smith, Drews and the other classics of this literature, but have to be content with giving out as new what has already been said.

So far, indeed, as these attempts are meant to serve the cause of historical truth, they can defend themselves by claiming that such a rapid acceptance throughout the Greek world of a faith which sprang out of Judaism, as is recorded in the traditional history of the beginnings of Christianity, is incomprehensible without further confirmation and that therefore a hearing may be claimed for the hypothesis of the derivation of Christianity from Greek thought. But the working out of this hypothesis is wrecked upon the fact that the Jesus of the two earlier Gospels has nothing whatever about Him which allows Him to be explained as a personality originating in a myth. Moreover, with His eschatological mode of thought He displays a peculiarity which a later period could not have given to a personality created by itself, for the good reason that in the generation before the destruction of Jerusalem by Titus it no longer possessed the knowledge of late-Jewish eschatology which was needed for that purpose. Again, what interest could the assumed mystery-religion of the Christ-cult have had in attributing to the pseudo-historical Jesus, invented by itself, a belief which had obviously remained unfulfilled, in an immediate end to the world and His revelation as the Son-of-Man-Messiah? By his eschatology Jesus is so completely and firmly rooted in the period in which the two oldest Gospels place Him, that He cannot possibly be represented as anything but a personality... which really appeared in that period. It is significant that those who dispute His historical existence very prudently take no account of the eschatological limitations of His thought and activities.

— *My Life and Thought*

The Mind of Jesus

As a result of Schweitzer's emphasis on the supremacy of eschatology in the thinking of Jesus, three writers, applying the newly fashionable vogue for psycho-pathology, published theories that Jesus suffered from one kind of mental abnormality or another: he had a tendency to delusions and hallucinations which amounted, they claimed, to paranoia, the definition of which was a good deal more chaotic than it is now. A Jesus, they felt, who believed in the coming of a practical Kingdom of God was obviously out of his mind. So for his medical degree Schweitzer chose to write a thesis entitled "A Psychiatric Study of Jesus."

In accordance with his principle of getting to the bottom of any subject he touched, Schweitzer read deeply about paranoia and other forms of psychosis, so far as they had then been studied, and took over a year writing his thesis. So his mistrust of psychoanalysis cannot be blamed, as it often is, on ignorance.

Indeed the opening paragraph of his thesis is actually a defense of the method, and puts the blame where it belongs, on imperfect practitioners.

So deeply did he believe in truth, including psychiatric truth, that he embarked on his analysis of his beloved Jesus with his eyes open to the possibility that he might in fact find genuine signs of mental disorder there.

As it turned out, however, he found no cause to alter his belief that Jesus was perfectly sane, no reason to suppose that the ethical genius sprang from an unbalanced vision; always assuming that he was, as Schweitzer insisted, a man sharing the life and thought of his time.

THE INNER SCHWEITZER

To those who knew him in public, Schweitzer appeared to be a confident, seemingly invulnerable thinker, writer, and speaker. His letters to Hélène during this period show a very different side to him: agonizingly sensitive, sure that some great destiny beckoned, but constantly unsure where to seek it. Without these letters, we would have little idea of the inner man, and our understanding would be much the poorer.

My Path

I am so tired and yet so quietly happy — alone on the last Sunday of Advent. All alone in the house.

Why am I that way, that I have an inner fear of all humans, even those who are close to me, afraid that they take my solitude away from me. There are only a few people to whom I have given the right, to share in my thoughts, with whom to have dialogue. But with those few I feel so rich.

... The room was dark, but a glimmer came from the street, and in the soft light I could recognize everything — vaguely.

This is how life lies ahead of me, the life I will spend in these rooms — dark yet brightened by a gentle, distant light — so be it — may God guide and bless me — I would like to know what it is — this God whom I implore — does he exist? — What is the spirit that forces me to follow my path — I who am not naive, but critical, not "humble" but "proud" — what do I know? Let us go on — the spirit that speaks to me is a *reality*, the only supernatural reality that really exists for me — the rest is only a symbol, based on the only reality: *I believe because I act* — that action is, for me, the essential reality — and while I act I will be both humble and proud — truthful as cutting steel.

To be humble — not only to have *the right and the strength* to be truthful — that is what I want — to proclaim the whole truth and to confirm it with my life, to gain strength from it — for this alone I sacrifice the happiness of life. You may tell me that this is a *self-delusion* — whatever: *I live from it*, I suffer with it, I cry, I laugh about it, I am *happy* about it. And as long as a few women of noble spirit support me with their fair sympathy, I can go my way alone.

—Letters to Hélène, December 21, 1902, and September 25, 1903

The Struggle for Lived Sermons

I was so unhappy on the way to the station. It was chaos; 25 sermons at once, and how to make a single one out of them.... And the fear of saying things that I have not explored enough ...to give a sermon which is "not lived"! I have been suffering from this since Tuesday....

That is why I spoke to you about my sermon almost with loathing. It is terrible — a terrible birth, when you bring your innermost thoughts into the world...when you must be a prophet and at the same time must say things as a curate....

—Letter to Hélène, January 30, 1904

Prescribed Texts

We preach about texts — prescribed texts — so we do not have to tell our own thoughts, and in the end we have run away from our own thoughts that we don't know any more. And one can only preach what is based on one's own thoughts. That this is not taught us in our pastoral training, I will hold against the professors forever. They shaped us into skilful practitioners, but did not want us to strive for something higher.

—Letter to Hélène, February 1905

The Eternal Body of Jesus

It is hardly an uplifting task to be a pastor in these days of doubt and indifference. One wishes to give the people of our time some spiritual encouragement, to bring them the message of Jesus, and that is not possible. The age wants its doubts dissolved without trouble or effort. But if the proclamation of the gospel were simply the dissolution of doubts and the defense of a doctrine, the preacher's would be the most taxing and thankless of tasks; that would be as though one were trying to enrich people's lives by straightening out their sums on a piece of paper. Fortunately it is not that at all — it is much, much finer. It is saying to people: "Do not stay where you are, but move ahead, move towards Jesus!" Do not ask yourself whether the road is firm or practicable, fit for the man who follows his inclinations, but look only to see that it is really the road that leads straight to Jesus. Peter is able to walk towards him, the moment he dismisses all human considerations....

How is Jesus alive for us? Do not attempt to prove his presence by formulations, even if they are sanctified by the ages. Of late I have very nearly lost my temper when some pious soul has come to me saying that no one can believe in the living presence of Jesus if they do not believe in his physical resurrection and the eternal existence of his glorified body. Jesus lives for everyone whom he directs, in matters great and small, as if he were here among us. He tells them "Do this or that." And they answer, quite simply, "Yes!" and go about their job, humble and busy.... The fact that the Lord still, in our days, gives his orders, proves to me — and for me it is the only proof — that he is neither a ghost nor dead, but that he lives.

If you will let me explain in my way this living presence, I will say to you: "The eternal body of Jesus is simply his words; for it was about them that he said 'Heaven and earth shall pass away, but my words shall not pass away!' "

— From a sermon preached on November 19, 1905

The Mighty Thought — Love

The mighty thought underlying the Beatitudes of the Sermon on the Mount, that we come to know God and belong to Him through love, Jesus introduces into the late-Jewish, Messianic expectation, without being in any way concerned to spiritualize those realistic ideas of the Kingdom of God and of blessedness. But the spirituality which lies in this religion of love must gradually, like a refiner's fire, seize upon all ideas which come into communication with it. Thus it is the destiny of Christianity to develop through a constant process of spiritualization....

The subject of all His preaching is love and, more generally, the preparation of the heart for the Kingdom.

— *My Life and Thought*

Duty

My duty — why can't I shake it off? After this distress, however, I feel peace again — not the sweet, passive peace, the confinement of the chained dog, but the proud peace of action. I know that my activity as I want to develop it with the renunciation of conventional happiness is necessary, not for myself, but for our time, and it will prove its merit only through renunciation. I feel that I do not deceive myself, that it is not some will o' the wisp idea that leads me astray; it is that quietest calm, the peace of a torn soul — you know that I hate St. Augustine, it is not the peace of a pious man: I am not pious. If I should come to the conclusion tomorrow that there is no god, and no immortality, and that morality is only an invention of society — that would not touch me at all. The equilibrium of my inner life and the knowledge of my duty would not be shaken in the least.

—Letter to Hélène, September 6, 1903

On Sin

I cannot speak to you about sin like those terrifying preachers of penitence who have arisen through the ages. And I would not wish to. They always remind me of those fearful storms which beat on the earth but give it none of the refreshment that a fine rain gives when the water, instead of falling in torrents and carrying all before it, gently penetrates the soil. John the Baptist was a powerful orator. But Jesus, speaking to the people gently, certainly touched them much more deeply and convinced them more deeply of their sin. Whoever speaks to others of guilt and sin should preach as a sinner; everything he says that is true is an episode from his own experience.

—From a sermon preached in St. Nicolai's Church, January 1912

The Pagan in Me

For me pagan thoughts coexist with the Christian, and I am not able to separate them. In all of us there is something pagan, something proud and grand that does not go well with Christianity, with the ideas of Christ because he did not know them. Have you noticed that in his parables he never mentions woods as we know them, as dark, mysterious, impenetrable, as they correspond to the equally dark, equally mysterious, and equally impenetrable character of us humans of the northern countries. Whenever I am in the woods, as soon as I hear their melodies, something that resides deeply in my heart, something pagan, yet religious, some feeling of pride and energy, of harshness and haughtiness that I cannot define.

—Letter to Hélène, January 30, 1904

The Sheep and the Goats

Sometimes it seems as if I had arrived beyond clouds and stars and could see the world in the most wonderful clarity. And therefore the right to be a heretic! To know only Jesus of Nazareth; to continue his work as the only religion, not to bear what Christianity has absorbed over the years in vulgarity. Not to be afraid of Hell, not to strive for the joys of Heaven, not to live in false fear, not the fake devotion that has become an essential part of our religion....

Last night before I went to sleep, I read the 25th chapter of the Gospel of St. Matthew because I especially love the verse: "Truly I tell you, just as you did it to one of the least of these who are my brothers, you did it to me." But when it came to the last judgment and the separation of the "sheep from the goats" I smiled: I do not want to belong to the sheep, and in heaven I would certainly meet quite a lot whom I do not like: St. Loyola, St. Hieronymus, and a few Prussian church leaders — and to be friendly with them, to exchange a brotherly kiss? No, I decline. Rather to Hell. There the crowd will be more congenial. With Julian Apostate, Caesar, Socrates, Plato, and Heraclitus one can have a fruitful conversation. Yes, I serve him, because of him, only because of him — because he is the only truth, the only happiness.

—Letter to Hélène, May 1, 1904

To Become Simply Human

Things are so strange in my life...I wanted to complete it in a small circle which I created for myself....It was to run its course in the shadow of the seminary tree which proclaimed spring and autumn to me when I was young. Now everything has turned out so completely differently, from an inner necessity, not from external causes....I must carry the glow of the Christmas lights into the world...become simply human...in order to serve the one who was human and is my Lord, although as I stand in His presence I am inwardly free in ideas and views...but through my Lord, through His great, pure will my life will become simple....

—Letter to Hélène, Christmas Eve, 1910

He Who Loses His Life Shall Find It

The destiny of man has to fulfil itself in a thousand ways, so that goodness may be actualized. What every individual has to contribute remains his own secret. But we must all mutually share in the knowledge that our existence attains its true value only when we have experienced in ourselves the truth of the declaration: "He who loses life shall find it."

—The Philosophy of Civilization

Optimism and Pessimism

To the question whether I am a pessimist or an optimist, I answer that my knowledge is pessimistic, but my willing and hoping are optimistic.   —My Life and Thought

The New Situation

We are no longer content like the generations before us, to believe in the Kingdom that comes of itself at the end of time.

Mankind today must either realize the Kingdom of God or perish. The very tragedy of our present situation compels us to devote ourselves in faith to its realization.

We are at the beginning of the end of the human race. The question before it is whether it will use for beneficial purposes or for purposes of destruction the power which modern science has placed in its hands. So long as its capacity for destruction was limited, it was possible to hope that reason would set a limit to disaster. Such an illusion is impossible today, when its power is illimitable. Our only hope is that the Spirit of God will strive with the spirit of the world and will prevail.

The last petition of the Lord's Prayer has again its original meaning for us as a prayer for deliverance from the dominion of the evil powers of the world. These are no less real to us as working in men's minds, instead of being embodied in angelic beings opposed to God. The first believers set their hope solely upon the Kingdom of God in expectation of the end of the world; we do it in expectation of the end of the human race.

But there can be no Kingdom of God in the world without the Kingdom of God in our hearts. The starting point is our determined effort to bring every thought and action under the sway of the Kingdom of God. Nothing can be achieved without inwardness. The Spirit of God will strive against the spirit of the world only when it has won its victory over that spirit in our hearts.

> —From the epilogue to E. N. Mozley, *The Theology of Albert Schweitzer for Christian Inquirers,* published in 1950, after the dropping of the atom bombs on Japan

2

Music and Its Meaning

Just as Schweitzer's life was suffused with Jesus, so it was also with music. In the great books on Bach, music and Jesus are inextricable, as they were for Bach himself. The summit of Bach's compositions, the Matthew Passion and the Mark Passion, are the putting into great music of his deep understanding of the suffering of Jesus as recounted in the Gospels. And the whole of Schweitzer's soul responded to this achievement. So deeply did he understand Bach that he was able single-handedly to reverse the opinion that had dominated both scholars and ordinary musicians, who had regarded Bach as a mechanical composer, and show him as a master of emotion.

From his childhood onward, we can see how sensitively Schweitzer responded to music, how frequently he was shattered by its power, and how right to the end of his life he used it as his relaxation and refreshment.

ENCOUNTERS WITH MUSIC

Childhood Feeling for Music

In my second school year we used to have a lesson in penmanship twice a week from the master who just before that gave a singing-lesson to the big boys. Now it happened one day that we had come over from the infant school too early, so that we had to wait outside the other classroom, and when they began the vocal duet, "In the mill by the stream below there I was sitting in quiet thought," followed by "Beautiful forest, who planted you there?" I had to hold on to the wall to prevent myself from falling. The charm of the two-part harmony of the songs thrilled me all over, to my very marrow, and similarly the first time I heard brass instruments playing together I almost fainted from excess of pleasure.

— Memoirs of Childhood and Youth

At a Concert Given by Marie-Joseph Erb

I was stunned to see his hands whirling around on the keyboard. And all by heart, without hesitation, without a mistake! I was lost in astonishment. With my modest knowledge of piano playing, I tried to figure out how he went to work to launch those cascades of arpeggios and those bursts of shooting stars, to make the melody come out so clearly, to achieve those pianissimi in which, nonetheless, not a single note was lost.

After the first piano pieces, which had kept me in a state of rapture, the artist rose, bowed as the entire assembly applauded, disappeared behind a door, came back when the applause did not die down, disappeared again, came back, disappeared. Finally there was silence. People studied the rest of the program. The women offered each other bonbons. I could not understand why all these people, having applauded so heartily, did not remain like me under the spell of what they had heard, and how they could resume their chatter.

But here was Mr. Erb, back again, smiling, and mounting the platform beside the singer. The latter had curls like those that young girls wore for their first communion, and carried long white gloves. She put a big bouquet of flowers on a chair, made a curtsy, opened her sheet of music, which trembled a bit in her hands, coughed lightly, looked at the pianist and made a slight sign with her head, to which he replied by beginning immediately the first measures of the accompaniment. I was very much aware of the beauty of the singing, but still my attention was especially attracted to the accompanist, who followed the singer so well when she accelerated or decreased the tempo, when she passed from pianissimo to fortissimo or returned from fortissimo to pianissimo. Never could I have imagined such flexibility. The display of virtuosity at the end took my breath away. It was for me a sudden revelation of the possibilities of the piano. On the way home I walked as in a dream.

The following days I worked on my scales and finger exercises and struggled with the Czerny studies with an unprecedented ardor, even when they were starred with sharps and double sharps, which I had so detested theretofore.

— "Un grand musicien français"

Beethoven

I finished everything and now I am *all alone. All alone* — that is glorious. I turned off the lamp and I followed the flickering of the fire in the stove and the sound of the church bells penetrated the November dusk. It is Saturday evening.

Then I went over to the piano and played Beethoven's sonata for the fortepiano. To perform for others is nothing, no — one has to be alone because one can rejoice, laugh, cry, and weep, — . Oh, this heavenly exuberance — and then this dreamy, blissful world which wafts through these transparent chords — and I was by myself — and it was glorious, glorious.

Is that selfish? Well — I don't care, it may be so — no, we were two, Beethoven and I. — How I thank you that you let me have a glimpse into your world [now addressing Beethoven] — in your beautiful, pain-torn, sun-drenched, peacefully dying world. How many have thanked you? How many will thank you? You great prophet of overcoming and of struggle for joyful serenity!   —Letter to Hélène, November 15, 1902

First Acquaintance with Bach and Wagner

It considerably helped my musical studies that Ernest Münch, a brother of my Mülhausen teacher, and himself organist of St. William's in Strasbourg..., entrusted to me the organ accompaniment of the Cantatas and the Passion music which were performed at them. Thus while I was still a young student I became familiar with Bach's creations and had an opportunity of dealing practically with the problems of the production today of the Master's Cantatas and Passion music.

St. William's Church in Strasbourg ranked at that time as one of the most important nurseries of the Bach cult which was coming into existence at the end of the last century. Ernest Münch had an extraordinary knowledge of the works of the Cantor of St. Thomas's. He was one of the first who abandoned the modernized rendering of the Cantatas and the Passion music which at the end of the nineteenth century was almost universal, and he strove for really artistic performances with his small choir accompanied by the famous Strasbourg orchestra. Many an evening did we sit over the scores of the Cantatas and the Passion music and discuss the right method of rendering them.

Together with my veneration for Bach went the same feeling for Richard Wagner. When I was a schoolboy at Mülhausen at the age of sixteen, I was allowed for the first time to go to the theater, and I heard there Wagner's *Tannhäuser*. This music overpowered me to such an extent that it was days before I was capable of giving proper attention to the lessons in school.

In Strasbourg, where the operatic performances conducted by Otto Lohse were of outstanding excellence, I had the opportunity of becoming thoroughly familiar with the whole of Wagner's works, except, of course, *Parsifal,* which at that time could only be performed at Bayreuth....

In October of this year [1893], the generosity of my father's elder brother, who was in business in Paris, secured for me the privilege of instruction on the organ from the Parisian organist Charles Marie Widor. My teacher at Mülhausen had brought me on so well that after hearing me play Widor took me as a pupil, although he normally confined his instruction to the members of the Organ Class at the Conservatoire. This instruction was for me an event of decisive importance. Widor led me on to a fundamental improvement of my technique and made me strive to attain to perfect plasticity in playing. At the same time there dawned on me, thanks to him, the meaning of the architectonic in music.   — *My Life and Thought*

The Start of the Bach Book

While busy with the *Quest of the Historical Jesus* I finished a book, written in French, on J. S. Bach. Widor, with whom I used to spend several weeks in Paris every spring, and frequently in the autumn too, had complained to me that there existed in French only biographical books about him, but none that provided any introduction to his art. I had to promise him that I would spend the autumn vacation of 1902 in writing an essay on the nature of Bach's art for the students of the Paris Conservatoire.

This was a task that attracted me because it gave me an opportunity of expressing thoughts at which I had arrived in the course of the close study of Bach, both theoretical and practical, entailed on me by my post as organist to the Bach Choir at St. Wilhelm's.

At the end of the vacation I had, in spite of the most strenuous work, not got further than the preliminary studies for the treatise. It had also become clear that this would expand into a book on Bach. With good courage I resigned myself to my fate.

— *My Life and Thought*

ON BACH

Bach and Religion

Music is an act of worship with Bach. His artistic activity and his personality are both based on his piety. If he is to be understood from any standpoint at all, it is from this. For him, art was religion and so had no concern with the world or with worldly success. It was an end in itself.

Bach includes religion in the definition of art in general. All great art, even secular, is in itself religious in his eyes; for him the tones do not perish but ascend to God like praise too deep to utter. — "Johann Sebastian Bach,"
in *Music in the Life of Albert Schweitzer*

Bach, the Musician Poet

In their fight against Wagner, the Anti-Wagnerites appealed to the ideal of classical music, as they had settled it to their own satisfaction. They defined it as pure music, accepting as such only music of which they believed they could say that it afforded no scope for poetical or pictorial aims, but was only concerned to give to beautiful lines of sound the most perfect existence possible. Bach, whose works in their completeness had been gradually getting better known, thanks to the edition produced by the Bach Society in the middle of the nineteenth century, was claimed by them on these principles, and Mozart as well, for this classical art of theirs, and they played him off against Wagner. His fugues seemed to them to be the incontrovertible proof that he served their ideal of pure music. He was depicted as a classic of this kind by Philip Spitta in his large, important three-volumed work in which he puts forward the biographical — and is the first to do so — on a foundation of penetrating research into the sources.

As a contrast to the Bach of these Guardians of the Grail of pure music I present the Bach who is a poet and painter in sound. All that lies in the text, the emotional and the pictorial alike, he strives to reproduce in the language of music with the utmost possible vitality and clearness. Before all else he aims at rendering the pictorial in lines of sound. He is even more tone-painter than tone-poet. His art is nearer to that of Berlioz than to that of Wagner. If the text speaks of drifting mists, of boisterous winds, of roaring rivers, of waves that ebb and flow, of leaves falling from the trees, of bells that ring for the dying, of the confident faith which walks with firm steps, or the weak faith that falters insecure, of the proud who will be abused, and the humble who will be exalted, of Satan rising in rebellion, of angels poised on the clouds of heaven, then one sees and hears all this in his music.

Bach has, in fact, at his disposal a language of sound. There are in his music constantly recurring rhythmical motives expressing peaceful blessedness, lively joy, intense pain, or pain sublimely borne.

The impulse to express poetic and pictorial plastic thoughts is of the essence of music. Music appeals to the creative imagination of the hearer, and endeavors to kindle into life in it the emotional experiences and the visions from which it came into being itself. But this it can do only if the person who uses the language of sound possesses the mysterious faculty of rendering thoughts with a clearness and definiteness surpassing its own natural power of expression. In this respect Bach is the greatest among the great.

His music is poetic and pictorial because its themes are born of poetic and pictorial ideas. Out of these themes the composition unfolds itself, a finished piece of architecture in lines of sound. What is in its essence poetic and pictorial music displays itself as Gothic architecture transformed into sound. What is greatest in this art, so full of natural life, so wonderfully plastic, and unique in the perfection of its form, is the spirit that breathes out from it. A soul which out of the world's unrest longs for peace and has itself already tasted peace allows others to share its own experience in this music.

It follows from the nature of Bach's art that, in order to produce its effects, it must be presented to the hearer in living and perfected plasticity. But this principle, which is fundamental for its worthy rendering, has even today to struggle for recognition. To begin with, it is a crime against the style of Bach's music that we perform it with huge orchestras and massed choirs. The Cantatas and the Passion music were written for choirs of twenty-five to thirty voices, and an orchestra of about the same number. Bach's orchestra does not accompany the choir, but is a partner with equal rights, and there is no such thing as an orchestral equivalent to a choir of a hundred and fifty voices. We shall therefore come to providing for the performance of Bach's music choirs of forty to fifty voices and orchestras of fifty to sixty instrumentalists. The wonderful interweaving of the voice parts must stand out, clear and distinct. For alto and soprano Bach did not use women's voices but boys' voices only, even for the solos. Choirs of male voices form a homogeneous whole. At the very least, then, women's voices should be supplemented with boys', but the ideal is that even the alto and soprano solos should be sung by boys.

Since Bach's music is architecture, the crescendos and decrescendos which in Beethoven's and post-Beethoven music are responses to emotional experiences are not appropriate. Alterations of forte and piano are significant in it only so far as they serve to emphasize leading phrases and to leave subsidiary ones less prominent. It is only within the limits of these alternations of forte and piano that declamatory crescendos and diminuendos are admissible. If they obliterate the difference between forte and piano, they ruin the architecture of the composition.

Since a Bach fugue always begins and ends with a main theme, it cannot tolerate any beginning and ending in piano.

Bach is played altogether too fast. Music which presupposes a visual comprehension of lines of sound advancing side by side becomes for the listener a chaos if a too rapid tempo makes this comprehension impossible.

Yet it is not so much by the tempo as by phrasing which makes the lines of sound stand out before the listener in a living plasticity, that it is made possible to appreciate the life which animates Bach's music.

Whereas down to the middle of the nineteenth century Bach, curiously enough, was generally played staccato, players have since that date gone to the other extreme of rendering him with a monotonous legato. That is how I learned to play him from Widor in 1893. But as time went on, it occurred to me that Bach calls for phrasing which is full of life. He thinks as a violinist. His notes are to be connected with each other and at the same time separated from each other in the way which is natural to the bow of a violin. To play well one of Bach's piano compositions means to render it as it would be performed by a string quartet.

Correct phrasing is to be secured by correct accenting. Bach demands that the notes which are decisive for the style of the line of sound's advance shall be given their full importance by the accenting. It is characteristic of the structure of his periods that as a rule they do not start from an accent but strive to reach one. They are conceived as beginning with an upward beat. It must, further, be noticed than in Bach the accents of the lines of sound do not as a rule coincide with the natural accents of the bars, but advance side by side with these in a freedom of their own. From this tension between the accents of the line of sound and those of the bars comes the extraordinary rhythmical vitality of Bach's music.

These are the external requirements for the rendering of Bach's music. But above and beyond them the music demands of us men and women that we attain a composure and an inwardness that will enable us to rouse to life something of the deep spirit which lies hidden within it.

— "Johann Sebastian Bach,"
in *Music in the Life of Albert Schweitzer*

Bach's Piety

One trait in the character of Bach is . . . the essential trait: Bach was a pious man. It was his piety that sustained him and kept him serene in his laborious existence. His scores, without any other document, would suffice to show us this; almost all of them carry at the head: "S.D.G.," Soli Deo Gloria. On the cover of the *Orgelbüchlein* the following verse may be read:

> Dem höchsten Gott allein zu Ehren,
> Dem Nächsten draus sich zu belehren.
>
> [For the honor of the most high God alone,
> And for the instruction of my neighbor.]

This deeply religious spirit is disclosed even in Friedemann's *Klavierbüchlein* at the top of the page where the first little pieces to play begin with the words "In Nomine Jesu." With anyone else these declarations of piety, scattered at every turn, and under the most insignificant circumstances, would appear exaggerated, if not affected. With Bach one feels that there is nothing there unnatural. Certainly here was a profound spirit; but profound not after the fashion of those who in a sort of jealous fear anxiously disclose to the public their internal life. There was something frank about his piety. He did not withdraw from it; it constituted an integral part of his artistic nature. If he embellished all his scores with his "S.D.G." it was because music was something essentially religious to him. It was after all the most powerful means of glorifying God; music as a secular accomplishment occupied only the second place. This fundamentally

religious conception of art is completely expressed in his definition of harmony. "The figured bass," he says in his course, "is
the most perfect foundation of music. It is executed with two
hands; the left hand plays the prescribed notes, and the right
hand adds consonances and dissonances in order that the whole
shall produce an agreeable harmony for the honor of God and
for the proper delight of the soul. Like all music, the figured
bass has no other purpose than the glory of God and the refreshment of the spirit; otherwise it is not true music, but a
diabolical and repetitious prattle [*ein teuflisches Geplerr und
Geleyer*]."

It was therefore wholly natural that he should speak in
a somewhat disdainful fashion of secular art. Witness the
proposal he made to Friedemann when he invited him to accompany him to the Dresden opera: "What do you say if we
should go again to listen to the pretty little songs of Dresden?"
But this did not prevent him from writing secular music and
even burlesque cantatas! In the last analysis this activity was
less a work of art for him than a pastime and a recreation for
his spirit.

This pious artist had a remarkable theological knowledge.
The theological works mentioned in the inventory certainly
enabled him to have opinions on the numerous dogmatic questions which were then agitating Protestantism. Did he not live
in that troubled epoch which followed the Reformation, in the
time of that second Reformation which arose, we know, at
the turn of the seventeenth and eighteenth centuries, and in
time was to produce a transformation in the spirit of Protestantism? The subjectivism in religion which had been restricted
within definite limits by Luther reappeared at that time in all its
strength in Spener, the leader of pietism.

...The struggle was engaged on all fronts. To speak the
truth, it was never to end; the same strained relations still
exist at this very moment between Protestant subjectivism and

the dogma adopted by the Reformation, between pietism and orthodoxy.

...At heart Bach was neither pietistic nor orthodox: he was a mystic thinker. Mysticism was the living spring from which sprang his piety. There are certain chorales and certain cantatas which make us feel more than elsewhere that the master has poured into them his soul. These are precisely the mystical chorales and cantatas. Like all the mystics, Bach, one may say, was obsessed by religious pessimism. This robust and healthy man, who lived surrounded by the affection of a great family, this man who was embodied energy and activity, who even had a pronounced taste for the frankly burlesque, felt at the bottom of his soul an intense desire, a *Sehnsucht,* for eternal rest. He knew, if any mortal ever did, what nostalgia for death was. Never elsewhere had this nostalgia for death been translated into music in a more impressive way. Many are the cantatas he wrote to describe the weariness of life. The moment the Gospels touch on the cherished idea, Bach seizes it and devotes to it a long description! All the cantatas for bass alone are in this sense mystical cantatas. They begin with the idea of weariness of life; then, little by little, the expectation of death quiets and illumines; in death Bach celebrates the supreme liberation, and describes in lovely spiritual lullabies the peace that at this thought invades his soul; or again, his happiness is translated into joyous and exuberant themes of a supernatural gaiety. We feel that his whole soul sings in this music, and that the believer has written it in a sort of exaltation. How powerful, moreover, is the impression! What a penetrating charm is in the admirable cradle song "Schlummert ein ihr müden Augen" [Fall asleep, you weary eyes], in the cantata "Ich habe genug" [I have had enough] (No. 82), or again in the simple melody "Komm, süsser Tod!" [Come, sweet death!].

So desired, so awaited, death did not at all surprise him. At the supreme moment his face must have been transfigured with that supernatural smile that we believe we can see in his cantatas and his mystical chorales.

— "Johann Sebastian Bach," in
Music in the Life of Albert Schweitzer

A Symphonic Day in the Jungle

Throughout his life Schweitzer never ceased to play and study Bach. In his jungle hospital he would improvise or play a little Bach every evening on his specially adapted piano with organ pedals. This had been presented to him by the Paris Bach Society and laboriously transported to Lambaréné, the final stages in a huge canoe and then up the hill by sheer human muscle.

Here is his humorous account of clearing the jungle with the help of relatives of patients and those patients near full recovery.

Without this humor, this exasperated forgiveness, how would his mind have maintained its balance and energy?

A day with these people moves on like a symphony.

Lento: They take very grumpily the axes and bush-knives that I distribute to them....In snail-tempo the procession goes to the spot where bush and tree are to be cut down. At last everyone is in his place. With great caution the first blows are struck.

Moderato: Axes and bush-knives move in extremely moderate time, which the conductor tries in vain to quicken. The midday break puts an end to the tedious movement.

Adagio: With much trouble I have brought the people back to the work place in the stifling forest. Not a breath of wind is stirring. One hears from time to time the stroke of an axe.

Scherzo: A few jokes, to which in my despair I tune myself up, are successful. The mental atmosphere gets livelier, merry words fly here and there, and a few begin to sing. It is now getting a little cooler too. A tiny gust of wind steals up from the river into the thick undergrowth.

Finale: All are jolly now. The wicked forest, on account of which they have to stand here instead of sitting comfortably in the hospital, shall have a bad time of it. Wild imprecations are hurled at it. Howling and yelling they attack it, axes and bush-knives vie with each other in battering it. But — no bird must fly up, no squirrel show itself, no question must be asked, no command given. With the very slightest distraction the spell would be broken. Then the axes and knives would come to rest, everybody would begin talking about what had happened or what they had heard, and there would be no getting them to work again.

Happily, no distraction comes. The music gets louder and faster. If this finale lasts even a good half-hour the day has not been wasted. And it continues till I shout "Amani! Amani!" (Enough! Enough!), and put an end to the work for the day.

— More from the Primeval Forest

3

Africa

Schweitzer's thirtieth birthday, January 14, 1905, was the date on which he had long planned that his life would change, when he would abandon the academic for the active life. So well had he kept the secret of his plan that even his closest friends had no idea what he had had in his mind for many years. Indeed, the only person who knew was Hélène Bresslau. Thanks to the ten-year correspondence between them she knew not only what he intended, but the long, painful struggles that he had had before making the final decision.

We get glimpses of those struggles in his letters to her. In his autobiography, My Life and Thought, he tells of his moment of decision in the fall of 1904. And in the magnificent sermon entitled "The Call to Mission," which he preached a week before his thirtieth birthday, he brought together the many themes that dominated his life, all now condensed into one tremendous statement of purpose — utterly down-to-earth and at the same time blazingly idealistic. Those who heard it, even those who knew him best, could not have known that he was telling them what he was going to do, and why. Reading it now, in the light of all that was to follow, we can see it as a wonderful illumination of his purpose, and we can judge how truthfully he was to bring that purpose to fruition.

What he intended was to go to central Africa as a medical missionary, and in this sermon he defines what he means — and what he does not mean — by this task.

Writing to his friend, the music critic Gustav von Lüpke, shortly before the sermon, he summarized the thoughts and feelings that drove him, and continued to drive him for the rest of his life.

THE REASON

For me the whole essence of religion is at stake. For me religion means to be human, plainly human in the sense in which Jesus was. In the colonies things are pretty hopeless and comfortless. We — the Christian nations — send out there the mere dregs of our people; we think only of what we can get out of the natives.... In short what is happening there is a mockery of humanity and Christianity. If this wrong is in some measure to be atoned for, we must send out there men who will do good in the name of Jesus, not simply proselytizing missionaries, but men who will help the distressed as they must be helped if the Sermon on the Mount and the words of Jesus are valid and right.

Now we sit here and study theology, and then compete for the best ecclesiastical posts, write thick learned books in order to become professors of theology...and what is going on out there where the honor and the name of Jesus are at stake does not concern us at all. And I am supposed to devote my life to making ever fresh critical discoveries, that I might become famous as a theologian and go on training pastors who will also sit at home, and will not have the right to send them out to this vital work. I cannot do so. For years I have turned these matters over in my mind, this way and that. At last it became clear to me that this isn't my life. I want to be a simple human being, doing something small in the spirit of Jesus.... "What you have done to the least of these my brethren you have done to me." Just as the wind is driven to spend its force in the big empty spaces so must the men who know the laws of the spirit go where men are most needed.

>   —Letter to music critic Gustav von Lüpke,
>   undated, quoted in Pierhal, *Albert Schweitzer*

The Call to Mission

Sermon preached on Sunday, January 6, 1905, at the morning service at St. Nicolai's Church.

> *And Jesus said unto them, Come ye after me, and I will make you to become fishers of men.*   (Mark 1:17)

On this day in the ancient church the Feast of the Epiphany was celebrated. It was the feast of the manifestation of Christ, the most ancient and most revered of festivals. Only later was it overshadowed by the Feast of Christmas, until finally it lost all its splendor. Celebrants of the Feast of Epiphany rejoiced in the revelation of Christ's glory on earth, his revelation as Savior.

In our country we keep our missionary festival this day, and rightly so. Of course it is not actually a festival, for festivals are celebrated in memory of some great event of the past. Here nothing done in the past is significant, for almost everything remains to be done. And nowadays there is very little to suggest a special celebration in our churches. Epiphany is no different from any ordinary Sunday.

Yet it is a festival. But it is very different from those noisy memorial days of which there are more than enough in our time, festivals in which the past is elevated to heaven and afterward everyone comes down to earth with a bump, when everything is turned back to front. Today is, rather, a com- memoration: we look forward, not remembering the past but looking to the present and the future, prepared to lend a hand in shaping what must come to be.

You have no more illusions than I about the popularity of missionary work. Even otherwise good and right-minded people shun any association with missions. I recently heard a gentleman in Paris who is much given to good works tell a lady who was collecting for a good cause, "Come at any time. You will always find an open door and an open hand. Only don't ever ask anything for missions. I never give a cent — it's money thrown down the drain."

Perhaps some of you don't regard missions very highly. You have never faced up to the subject properly.

Consider my own experience over the past few years. How often I have got into an argument about missions — over land and sea, traveling by road and by train, on mountaintops and in the plains, with friends and with strangers. I make it a matter of principle never to allow a thoughtless remark about missions to pass unnoticed in my presence. Thus I have a pretty good idea why people are so opposed to missions.

I want to tell you my reason for standing up for missions — just a few words to counteract some people's prejudices maybe, but especially that you may know how to reply if somebody should ever say anything against missions in your presence. If ever a preacher who Sunday by Sunday lays bare his thoughts and his heart has the right to ask you for something, I now ask you this one thing. Never permit in your presence any thoughtless talk or grumbling about missionary work. Never allow such opinions to go unanswered.

The first objection we always hear is this: Why don't you leave people to their own religion? Uprooting them from the faiths which until now have made them happy only disturbs them. To this I reply: for me, missionary work in itself is not primarily a religious matter. Far from it. It is first and foremost a duty of humanity never realized or acted upon by our

states and nations. Only religious people, only simple souls,
have undertaken it in the name of Jesus.

What do our people and nations think about when they gaze
across the sea? Of countries to be taken under their so-called
protection or otherwise annexed? Of what they might siphon
out of the country — always to their advantage? But how they
can make those human beings really human, how they can teach
them to work and acquire civilization, how civilizations can be
developed so that contact with other cultures does not destroy
them — that is something these states never consider. Our own
states, with all the culture they boast, look very different from
the other viewpoint. We are robber states. And where are the
people in our civilized states who will undertake long-term, self-
less labor to educate other peoples and bring them the blessings
of our culture? Where are the workmen, tradesmen, teachers,
professors, and doctors who will go to these countries and work
there to achieve the blessings of culture? What efforts does our
society make in that direction? None at all. Only a few poor
missionaries with all their limitations have undertaken a work
that our whole society should have been eager to do. Missionaries, not the heads of our elegant and boastful culture, deserve
the laurel wreath. They have worked humanly for decades to
raise the standards of other people, without primarily giving
thought to making their religion understood.

Why? Because to be a disciple of Jesus is the only culture in
which a human being is always a human being, always someone who has a right to the assistance and sacrifice of his fellow
men. But our culture divides people into two classes: civilized
men, a title bestowed on the persons who do the classifying;
and others, who have only the human form, who may perish or
go to the dogs for all the "civilized men" care.

Oh, this "noble" culture of ours! It speaks so piously of
human dignity and human rights and then disregards this dignity and these rights of countless millions and treads them
underfoot, only because they live overseas or because their skins

are of different color or because they cannot help themselves. This culture does not know how hollow and miserable and full of glib talk it is, how common it looks to those who follow it across the seas and see what it has done there, and this culture has no right to speak of personal dignity and human rights. Until culture wakes up to its own mission and does something about it, let no one say a word against missions. Missionaries were the ones who stepped in and did their best. True religion is also true humanitarianism. So the missions stepped into the breach for our culture, for our civilization, for our society — and they did for other people what all the other agencies should have done.

If someone were to ask me why I consider Christianity to be the highest and only religion, I would discard all we have learned about comparative religions and their relative worth, and how to judge the strong points of each, and I would say only this: The first command the Lord gave upon earth can be condensed to only one word: man. He does not speak of religion, of faith, of the soul, or of any thing else on earth; he speaks only of man. "I will make you fishers of men." It is as though he were speaking to all centuries to come: First see to it, I beg you, that man does not perish. Go after him as I went after him and find him where he is, where others have not found him, in filth, in neglect, in indignity. Live with him and help him to become man again.

Jesus has welded religion and humanity so closely together that religion no longer exists as a separate entity; without true humanity, there is no religion. And the challenge of true humanity can no longer be heard without religion.

This human appreciation of missions must prevail. You must stand up for it and labor so that it will prevail. Many of the objections against missionary work will then fall to the ground.

People say there is still so much to be done at home that missionary work should wait until everything has been accomplished here. There are enough heathens to be converted at home, so I will wait until we have supplied the missionary effort with more skilled people than I can actually afford.

A man once said to me, "We need money for all the good that needs to be done at home. I won't give a dime for missionary work." Knowing him well, I asked him whether he gave more for good causes at home, since he did not send anything abroad, and how much he contributed every year to these worthy causes. We continued our walk, and he remained silent. So did I. But since then, the missions have been getting money from him.

What should we answer when they say that missionary work doesn't do any good, that it only squanders money and manpower for nothing? Of course one could tell a long story about the successes of missionary work. One could tell of its accomplishments in the Great Lakes District of Central Africa, what it has done in the South Sea Islands, the hundreds and hundreds of busy, untroubled villages it has created, how it has put a stop to bloodshed, and much more than that. But no. For missionary work is carried on without thought of success. It goes on because it must, out of a compelling force that is the very nature of things where the Spirit of Jesus is.

Ordinary men in everyday life calculate the chances of success; they will undertake a project only if they are confident of reward. But when something is done in Jesus' name, the only thing to take into account is the "must," that mysterious "must" that Jesus keeps insisting on when he talks of the destiny of the Son of man, of the death that awaited him. The less our prospect of success, the greater the force of that "must."

So let us not be sparing in our contributions in money or manpower. Nothing will ever be wasted. And even if it should be buried in the sea or in the desert, it will still be hallowed by the death of Jesus. His death removed the sting from those painful words: "in vain." When he died, men could say, "This person threw himself away and lived in vain" — and yet out of his death came strength. All that is done while following in his footsteps, the effort that seems to be done in vain bears sacred fruit a thousandfold.

Finally, missionary work is simply an atonement for the crimes of violence done in the name of Christian nations. I will not enumerate all the crimes that have been committed under the pretext of justice. People robbed native inhabitants of their land, made slaves of them, let loose the scum of mankind upon them. Think of the atrocities that were perpetrated upon people made subservient to us, how systematically we have ruined them with our alcoholic "gifts," and everything else we have done. What have the German people done in South West Africa to bring about this revolt? What are we doing now? We decimate them, and then, by the stroke of a pen, we take their land so they have nothing left at all.

I will not discuss this, for I always get the reply: "Well, it could not be helped. In this world, force rules."

All right, but if all this oppression and all this sin and shame are perpetrated under the eye of the German God, or the American God, or the British God, and if our states do not feel obliged first to lay aside their claim to be "Christian" — then the name of Jesus is blasphemed and made a mockery. And the Christianity of our states is blasphemed and made a mockery before those poor people. The name of Jesus has become a curse, and our Christianity — yours and mine — has become a falsehood and a disgrace, if the crimes are not atoned for in the very place where they were instigated. For every person who committed an atrocity in Jesus' name, someone must step in to help in Jesus' name; for every person who robbed, someone must bring a replacement; for everyone who cursed, someone must bless.

In two years about 15,000 troops of the Christian German Empire were sent out among the blacks. About 1,500 died. When will we, the Christian Germany, send out there 15,000 fighters for Jesus, the Lord of mankind? Only then will our name of "Christian" be redeemed — a little, anyhow.

Once, in the mid-nineties, Professor Lucius, a devoted friend of missions who died tragically at a young age, was lecturing about the history of missions on a summer afternoon between three and four o'clock. It was very hot, and barely a half dozen students were present. In his words that day I heard, for the first time, the idea of atonement.

It was so strange. Dogmatics and New Testament exegesis found it difficult to explain why Jesus died for the sins of the world. Everything we had been told about the crucifixion was cut and dried, lifeless. And we could tell that those who lectured on the subject were not too confident about its meaning themselves. But now, as a call to service in Jesus' name, the significance of missions became alive. The word cried so loudly that we could not escape understanding and grasping it. And from that day on, I understood Christianity better and knew why we must work in the mission field.

And now, when you speak about missions, let this be your message: We must make atonement for all the terrible crimes we read of in the newspapers. We must make atonement for the still worse ones, which we do not read about in the papers, crimes that are shrouded in the silence of the jungle night. Then you preach Christianity and missionary work at the same time. I implore you to preach it.

— Sermon preached at St. Nicolai's Church,
January 6, 1905

Six months later Schweitzer wrote to the Paris Missionary Society, offering himself as a candidate for a post with them.

Job-Seeker's Jitters

There followed a period when it seemed that it was never going to work, when he suffered the usual agonies of job-seekers when it seemed that he would get no reply to his application to the Paris Missionary Society, and then endless obstacles due to his unorthodox theology. Again it is good to be reminded of his vulnerable humanity, and also, as he himself used to say later, that it was not really a hardship to go to Africa. The real hardship would have been to continue with the academic life that had come to suffocate him.

My hand shakes a little: I just put the letter in the mailbox in which I tell the Director of the Paris Mission that I am ready and willing to leave in February 1910. The letter has been written: clear, precise, without any sentiments, almost like a business letter. I carried it to the mailbox; when I returned I stood still for a moment and looked at the two towers of the Thomas church which stood above the courtyard enveloped in a soft light...I am happy. It is done. I am not afraid that I might regret anything. — Letter to Hélène, July 9, 1905

My head aches. I had a restless night, and this morning I feel as if my soul does not live in my body. It follows my letter, wants to bring it back; wants to be free again to decide, to make the decision. — Letter to Hélène, July 10, 1905

I am desolate, it is almost an attack of despair. I wait in vain for an answer from Paris...every morning I wake up and wait for the mail — nothing; at eleven o'clock again — nothing. Today on my way to the confirmation class...the eleven o'clock mailman shook his head again....I felt like breaking my cane on the railing of the bridge and throwing it into the water.
— Letter to Hélène, July 20, 1905

Today we had our Faculty meeting...when the program of courses was determined, I thought with a shudder that perhaps I might have spent my whole life preparing course schedules.
— Letter to Hélène, December 18, 1905

From a letter to Hélène after meeting with real missionaries who had worked in Africa, as opposed to the Mission Society Committee in Paris:

These men are simple and of great depth. No veneer. One of them asked with a sad voice, whether there was anybody in this assembly who would come and help him in the Congo.... If there is an invisible communication between souls, he must have heard my Yes.   —Letter to Hélène, October 12, 1905

The moment of decision, the thoughts and events that led up to it, and its consequences, are summed up in the following section.

The Decision

On October 13, 1905, a Friday, I dropped into a letter-box in the Avenue de la Grande Armée in Paris letters to my parents and to some of my most intimate acquaintances, telling them that at the beginning of the winter term I should enter myself as a medical student, in order to go later on to Equatorial Africa as a doctor. In one of them I sent in the resignation of my post as Principal of the Theological College of St. Thomas's, because of the claim on my time that my intended course of study would make.

The plan which I meant now to put into execution had been in my mind for a long time, having been conceived as long ago as my student days. It struck me as incomprehensible that I should be allowed to lead such a happy life, while I saw so many people around me wrestling with care and suffering. Even at school I had felt stirred whenever I got a glimpse of the miserable home surroundings of some of my school-fellows and compared them with the absolutely ideal conditions in which we children of the parsonage at Günsbach lived. While at the university and enjoying the happiness of being able to study and even to produce some results in science and art, I could not help thinking continually of others who were denied that happiness by their material circumstances or their health. Then one brilliant summer morning at Günsbach, during the Whitsuntide holidays — it was in 1896 — there came to me, as I awoke, the thought that I must not accept this happiness as a matter of course, but must give something in return for it. Proceeding to think the matter out at once with calm deliberation, while the birds were singing outside, I settled with myself before I got up that I would consider myself justified in living till I was thirty for science and art, in order to devote myself from that time forward to the direct service of humanity. Many a time already had I tried to settle what meaning lay hidden for me in the saying of Jesus, "Whosoever would save his life shall lose it, and whosoever shall lose his life for My sake and the Gospels shall save it"! Now the answer was found. In addition to the outward, I now had inward happiness.

What would be the character of the activities thus planned for the future was not yet clear to me. I left it to circumstances to guide me. One thing only was certain, that it must be directly human service, however inconspicuous the sphere of it.

•

One morning in the autumn of 1904 I found on my writing table in the College one of the green-covered magazines in which the Paris Missionary Society reported every month on its activities. A certain Miss Scherdlin used to put them there, knowing that I was specially interested in this Society on account of the impression made on me by the letters of one of its earliest missionaries, Casalis by name, when my father read them aloud at his missionary services during my childhood. That evening in the very act of putting it aside that I might go on with my work, I mechanically opened this magazine, which had been laid on my table during my absence. As I did so, my eye caught the title of an article, "The Needs of the Congo Mission."

It was by Alfred Boegner, the president of the Paris Missionary Society, an Alsatian, and contained a complaint that the Mission had not enough workers to carry on its work in the Gabon, the northern province of the Congo Colony. The writer expressed his hope that his appeal would bring some of those "on whom the Master's eyes already rested" to a decision to offer themselves for this urgent work. The conclusion ran: "Men and women who can reply simply to the Master's call, 'Lord, I am coming,' those are the people whom the church needs." The article finished, I quietly began my work. My search was over.

•

My relatives and my friends all joined in expostulating with me on the folly of my enterprise. I was a man, they said, who was burying the talent entrusted to him and wanted to trade with false currency. Work among savages I ought to leave to those who would not thereby be compelled to leave gifts and acquirements in science and art unused. Widor, who loved me as if I were his son, scolded me as being like a general who wanted to go into the firing-line...with a rifle.

In the many verbal duels which I had to fight, as a weary opponent, with people who passed for Christians, it moved me strangely to see them so far from perceiving that the effort to serve the love preached by Jesus may sweep a man into a new course of life, although they read in the New Testament that it can do so, and found it there quite in order. I had assumed as a matter of course that familiarity with the sayings of Jesus would produce a much better appreciation of what to popular logic is non-rational, than my own case allowed me to assert. Several times, indeed, it was my experience that my appeal to the act of obedience which Jesus' command of love may under special circumstances call for, brought upon me an accusation of conceit, although I had, in fact, been obliged to do violence to my feelings to employ this argument at all. In general, how much I suffered through so many people assuming a right to tear open all the doors and shutters of my inner self!

... They thought there must be something behind it all, and guessed at disappointment at the slow growth of my reputation. ... Unfortunate love experiences were also alleged as the reason for my decision.

I felt as a real kindness the action of persons who made no attempt to dig their fists into my heart, but regarded me as a precocious young man, not quite right in the head, and treated me correspondingly with affectionate mockery.

I felt it to be, in itself, quite natural that relations and friends should put before me anything that told against the reason-ableness of my plan. As one who demands that idealists shall be sober in their views, I was conscious that every start upon an untrodden path is a venture which only in unusual circum-stances looks sensible and likely to be successful. In my own case I held the venture to be justified, because I had considered it for a long time and from every point of view, and credited myself with the possession of health, sound nerves, energy, prac-tical common sense, toughness, prudence, very few wants, and everything else that might be found necessary by anyone wan-dering along the path of the idea. I believed myself, further, to wear the protective armor of a temperament quite capable of enduring an eventual failure of my plan.

•

What seemed to my friends the most irrational thing in my plan was that I wanted to go to Africa, not as a missionary, but as a doctor, and thus when already thirty years of age burdened myself as a first step with a long period of laborious study. And that this study would mean for me a tremendous effort, I had no manner of doubt. I did, in truth, look forward to the next few years with dread. But the reasons which determined me to follow the way of service I had chosen, as a doctor, weighed so heavily that other considerations were as dust in the balance.

I wanted to be a doctor that I might be able to work without having to talk. For years I had been giving myself out in words, and it was with joy that I had followed the calling of theological teacher and of preacher. But this new form of activity I could not represent to myself as being talking about the religion of love, but only as an actual putting it into practice. Medical knowledge made it possible for me to carry out my intention in the best and most complete way, wherever the path of service might lead me. In view of the plan for Equatorial Africa, the acquisition of such knowledge was especially indicated because in the district to which I thought of going as a doctor was, according to the missionaries' reports, the most needed of all needed things. They were always complaining in their magazine that the natives who visited them in physical suffering could not be given the help they desired. To become one day the doctor whom these poor creatures needed, it was worthwhile, so I judged, to become a medical student.

There was still one more point of view from which I seemed directed to become a doctor. From what I knew of the Paris Missionary Society, I could not but feel it to be very doubtful whether they would accept me as a missionary....

It was always interesting to me to find that the missionaries themselves usually thought more liberally than the officials of their societies. They had, of course, found by experience that among outside peoples, especially among the primitive races, there is a complete absence of those presuppositions which compel our Christianity at home to face the alternative of doctrinal constraint or doctrinal freedom, and that the important thing out there is to preach the elements of the Gospel as given in the Sermon on the Mount, and to bring men under the lordship of the spirit of Jesus....   — My Life and Thought

TO AFRICA

The Journey

*A storm in the Bay of Biscay lasted three days. Schweitzer, un-
prepared, had not made the baggage fast, and in the night the
cabin trunks*

... began to chase each other about. The two hat cases also,
which contained our sun-helmets, took part in the game without reflecting how badly off they might come in it, and when I
tried to catch the trunks, I nearly got one leg crushed between
them and the wall of the cabin. So I left them to their fate and
contented myself with lying quietly in my berth and counting
how many seconds elapsed between each plunge made by the
ship and the corresponding rush of our boxes. Soon there could
be heard similar noises from other cabins and added to them
the sound of crockery, etc., moving wildly about in the galley
and the dining saloon.

— On the Edge of the Primeval Forest

*Then, at last, Africa — the Gabon (French Equatorial Africa)
and the Ogowe River:*

River and forest...! Who can really describe the first impression they make? We seemed to be dreaming! Pictures of
antediluvian scenery which elsewhere had seemed to be merely
the creation of fancy are now seen in real life. It is impossible to
say where the river ends and the land begins, for a mighty net-
work of roots, clothed with bright-flowering creepers, projects
right into the water. Clumps of palms and palm trees, ordinary
trees spreading out widely with green boughs and huge leaves,
single trees of the pine family shooting up to a towering height
in between them, wide fields of papyrus clumps as tall as a man,
with big fan-like leaves, and amid all this luxuriant greenery the

rotting stems of dead giants shooting up to heaven.... In every gap in the forest a water mirror meets the eye; at every bend in the river a new tributary shows itself. A heron flies heavily up and then settles on a dead tree trunk; white birds and blue birds skim over the water, and high in the air a pair of ospreys circle. Then — yes; there can be no mistake about it — from the branch of a palm there hang and swing — two monkey tails! Now the owners of the tails are visible. We are really in Africa!

So it goes on, hour by hour. Each new corner, each new bend, is like the last. Always the same forest and the same yellow water. The impression which nature makes on us is immeasurably deepened by the constant monotonous repetition. You shut your eyes for an hour, and when you open them you see exactly what you saw before. The Ogowe is not a river but a river system, three or four branches, each as big as the Rhine, twisting themselves together, and in between are lakes big and little. How the black pilot finds his way through this maze of watercourses is a riddle to me.

— *On the Edge of the Primeval Forest*

LAMBARÉNÉ

The First Hospital

The Lambaréné mission station is built on hills, the one which lies farthest upstream having on its summit the buildings of the boys' school, and on the side which slopes down to the river the storehouse and the largest of the mission houses. On the middle hill is the doctor's little house, and on the remaining one the girls' school and the other mission house. Some twenty yards beyond the houses is the edge of the forest. We live, then, between the river and the virgin forest, on three hills, which every year have to be secured afresh against the invasion of wild Nature, who is ever trying to get her own back again. All round the houses there are coffee bushes, cocoa trees, lemon trees, orange trees, mandarin trees, mango trees, oil palms, and paw-paw trees. To the natives its name has always been "Andende." Deeply indebted are we to the first missionaries that they took so much trouble to grow these big trees.

The station is about 650 yards long and 110 to 120 yards across. We measure it again and again in every direction in our evening and Sunday constitutionals, which one seldom or never takes on the paths that lead to the nearest villages. On these paths the heat is intolerable, for on either side of these narrow passages rises the forest in an impenetrable wall nearly 100 feet high, and between these walls not a breath of air stirs. There is the same absence of air and movement in Lambaréné. One seems to be living in a prison. If we could only cut down a corner of the forest which shuts in the lower end of the station we should get a little of the breeze in the river valley; but we have neither the money nor the men for such an attack on the trees. The only relief we have is that in the dry season the river sand-banks are exposed, and we can take our exercise upon them and enjoy the breeze which blows upstream.

— On the Edge of the Primeval Forest

The average shade temperature in the rainy season is 82°–86°F. (28°–30°C.), in the dry season about 77°–82°F. (25°–28°C.), the nights being always nearly as hot as the days. This circumstance, and the excessive moisture of the atmosphere, are the chief things which make the climate of the Ogowe lowlands such a trial for a European. After a year's residence fatigue and anemia begin to make themselves disagreeably perceptible. At the end of two or three years he becomes incapable of real work, and does best to return to Europe for at least eight months in order to recruit.

In 1903, the mortality among the whites at Libreville, the capital of the Gabon, was 14 percent. . . .

Before the war there were about two hundred whites in the Ogowe lowlands: planters, timber merchants, storekeepers, officials, and missionaries. The number of the natives is hard to estimate, but, at any rate, the country is not thickly inhabited. We have at present merely the remains of eight once powerful tribes, so terribly has the population been thinned by three hundred years of alcohol and the slave trade.

—*My Life and Thought*

At Lambaréné the missionaries gave us a very hearty welcome. They had unfortunately not been able to erect the little buildings of corrugated iron in which I was to begin my medical activity, for they had not secured the necessary laborers. The trade in okoume wood, which was just beginning to flourish in the Ogowe district, offered any native who was fairly capable better-paid work than he could find on the mission station. So at first I had to use as my consulting room an old fowl-house close to our living quarters, but in the late autumn I was able to move to a corrugated-iron building down by the river, twenty-six feet long and thirteen feet wide, with a roof of palm-leaves. It contained a small consulting room, an operation room of similar proportions, and a still smaller dispensary. Round about this building there gradually came into existence a number of large bamboo huts for the accommodation of the native patients. The white patients found quarters in the mission house and in the doctor's little bungalow.   —*My Life and Thought*

From the very first days, before I had even found time to unpack the drugs and instruments, I was besieged by sick people. The choice of Lambaréné as the site of the hospital had been made on the strength of the map and of the facts given us by Mr. Morel, the missionary, a native of Alsace, and it proved to be in every respect a happy one. From a distance of one or two hundred miles around, from upstream or downstream, the sick

could be brought to me in canoes along the Ogowe and its efflu-
ents. The chief diseases I had to deal with were malaria, leprosy,
sleeping sickness, dysentery, framboesia, and phagedenic ulcers,
but I was surprised at the number of cases of pneumonia and
heart disease which I discovered. There was much work too
with urinary diseases. Surgical treatment was called for chiefly
by hernia and elephantiasis tumors. Hernia is much commoner
among the natives in Equatorial Africa than among us white
people. If there is no medical man in the neighborhood, every
year sees a number of unfortunate mortals doomed to die a
painful death from strangulated hernia from which a timely operation might have saved them. My first surgical intervention
was in a case of that kind.

Thus I had during the very first weeks full opportunity for
establishing the fact that physical misery among the natives is
not less but even greater than I had supposed. How glad I was
that in defiance of all objections I had carried out my plan of
going out there as a doctor. . . .

At first I was much hindered in my work by being unable
to find natives who could serve as interpreters and orderlies.
The first who showed himself worth anything was one who had
been a cook, Joseph Azoawani by name, who stayed with me,
though I could not pay him as much as he had earned in his former calling. He gave me some valuable hints about how to deal
with the natives, though upon the one which he thought the
most important I was unable to act. He advised me to refuse as
patients those whose lives, so far as we could see, we were not
likely to save. Again and again he held up to me the example
of the fetish doctors who would have nothing to do with such
cases in order to endanger as little as possible their reputation
as healers.

But on one point I had later to admit that he was right. One
must never, when dealing with natives, hold out hopes of recovery to the patient and his relatives, if the case is really hopeless.
If death occurs without warning of it having been given, it is

concluded that the doctor did not know the disease would have this outcome because he had not diagnosed it correctly. To native patients one must tell the truth without reservation. They wish to know it and they can endure it, for death is to them something natural. They are not afraid of it, but face it calmly. If after all the patient unexpectedly recovers, so much the better for the doctor's reputation. He ranks thereafter as one who can cure even fatal diseases.

Valiant help was given in the hospital by my wife, who had been trained as a nurse. She looked after the severe cases, superintended the linen and the bandages, was often busy in the dispensary, kept the instruments in proper condition, made all the preparations for the operations, herself then administering the anesthetics, while Joseph acted as assistant. That she successfully managed the complicated work of an African household and yet could find every day some hours to spare for the hospital was really a wonderful achievement.

Fortunately I did not lose a single one of those patients on whom I first operated.

At the end of a few months of work the hospital had to find every day accommodation for about forty patients. I had, however, to provide shelter not only for these but for the companions who had brought them long distances in canoes, and who stayed with them in order to paddle them back home again.

The actual work, heavy as it was, I found a lighter burden than the care and responsibility which came with it. I belong unfortunately to the number of those medical men who have not the robust temperament which is desirable in that calling, and so are consumed with unceasing anxiety about the condition of their severe cases and of those on whom they have operated. In vain have I tried to train myself to that equanimity which makes it possible for a doctor, in spite of all his sympathy with the sufferings of his patients, to husband, as is desirable, his spiritual and nervous energy....

In my intercourse with the natives I naturally came to put to myself the much debated question whether they were mere prisoners of tradition, or beings capable of really independent thought. In the conversations I had with them I found to my astonishment that they were far more interested in the elementary questions about the meaning of life and the nature of good and evil than I had supposed.

As I had expected, the questions of dogma on which the Missionary Society's committee in Paris had laid so much weight played practically no part in the sermons of the missionaries. If they wanted to be understood by their hearers they could do nothing beyond preaching the simple Gospel of becoming freed from the world by the spirit of Jesus, the Gospel which comes to us in the Sermon on the Mount and the finest sayings of St. Paul. Necessity compelled them to put forward Christianity as before all else an ethical religion. When they met each other at the mission conferences held twice a year now at this station, now at that, their discussions bore on the problems of how to secure practical Christianity in their district, not on doctrinal ones. That in matters of belief some of them thought more strictly than others played no part in the missionary work, which they carried on in common. As I did not make the smallest attempt to foist any theological views upon them, they soon laid aside all mistrust of me and rejoiced, as did I also on my side, that we were united in the piety of obedience to Jesus and in the will to simple Christian activity. Not many months after my arrival I was invited to take part in the preaching and thus was released from the promise I had given in Paris "d'être muet comme une carpe" — "to be as dumb as a carp...."

I found preaching a great joy. It seemed to me a glorious thing to be allowed to preach the sayings of Jesus and Paul to people to whom they were quite new. As interpreters I had the native teachers of the Mission School, who translated each sentence at once into the language of the Galoas or of the Pahuins, or sometimes into both in succession.

— *My Life and Thought*

Joseph

It would have doubled Schweitzer's problems if he had not had a reliable African assistant, and one who could guide him through the intricacies of local customs and beliefs. Joseph was truly a godsend and stayed loyally with Schweitzer for many years — two men whose mutual respect and admiration made for effective, if somewhat comical, teamwork.

Among my patients there turned up a very intelligent-looking native, who spoke French remarkably well, and said he was a cook by trade but had had to give up that kind of work as it disagreed with his health. I asked him to come to us temporarily, as we could not find a cook, and at the same time to help me as interpreter and surgical assistant. His name was Joseph, and he proved extremely handy. It was hardly surprising that, as he had acquired his knowledge of anatomy in the kitchen, he should, as a matter of habit, use kitchen terms in the surgery: "This man's right leg of mutton (gigot) hurts him." "This woman has a pain in her upper left cutlet, and in her loin!" At the end of May N'Zeng arrived, the man whom I had written to engage beforehand, but as he did not seem to be very reliable, I kept Joseph on...

•

That Joseph can allow himself to collect the vessels with blood in them after an operation and to wash the instruments is a sign of very high enlightenment. An ordinary African will touch nothing that is defiled with blood or pus, because it would make him unclean in the religious sense. In many districts of Equatorial Africa it is difficult, or even impossible, to persuade the natives to let themselves be operated on, and why those on the Ogowe even crowd to us for the purpose I do not know. Their readiness is probably connected with the fact that some years ago an army doctor, Jorryguibert by name, stayed some time with the District Commandant at Lambaréné and performed a series of successful operations. He sowed, and I am reaping.

•

I am always able to rely on Joseph. True, he can neither read nor write, but in spite of that he never makes a mistake when he has to get a medicine down from the shelf. He remembers the look of the words on the label, and reads this, without knowing the individual letters. His memory is magnificent, and his capacity for languages remarkable. He knows well eight African dialects, and speaks fairly well both French and English. He is at present a single man, as his wife left him, when he was a cook down on the coast, to go and live with a white man. The purchase price of a new life companion would be about 600 francs (£24), but the money can be paid in installments. Joseph, however, has no mind to take another wife under these conditions, for he thinks they are an abomination. "If one of us," he said to me, "has not completely paid for his wife, his life is most uncomfortable. His wife does not obey him, and whenever an opportunity offers she taunts him with having no right to say anything to her, because she has not yet been paid for."

As Joseph does not understand how to save any better than the other natives, I have bestowed on him a money-box in which to save up for the purchase of a wife. Into this goes all his extra pay for sitting up at night or other special services, and all the tips he gets from white patients.

— *On the Edge of the Primeval Forest*

Diseases at Lambaréné

In the first nine months of my work here I had close on two thousand patients to examine, and I can affirm that most European diseases are represented here; I even had a child with whooping-cough. Cancer, however, and appendicitis I have never seen. Apparently they have not yet reached the natives of Equatorial Africa. On the other hand, chills play a great part here. At the beginning of the dry season there is as much sneezing and coughing in the church at Lambaréné as there is in England at a midnight service on New Year's Eve. Many children die of unrecognized pleurisy.

In the dry season the nights are fresher and colder than at other times, and as the natives have no bed-clothes they get so cold in their huts that they cannot sleep, even though, according to European standards, the temperature is still fairly high. On cold nights the thermometer shows at least 68°F., but the damp of the atmosphere, which makes people sweat continually by day, makes them thereby so sensitive that they shiver and freeze by night. White people, too, suffer continually from chills and colds in the head, and there is much truth in a sentence I came across in a book on tropical medicine, though it seemed at the time rather paradoxical: "Where the sun is hot, one must be more careful than elsewhere to avoid chills." Especially fatal to the natives is the camp life on the sandbanks when they are out on their summer fishing expeditions. Most of the old folk die of pneumonia which they have caught on these occasions.

Rheumatism is commoner here than in Europe, and I not infrequently come across cases of gout, though the sufferers cannot be said to bring it on by an epicurean diet. That they eat too much flesh food cannot possibly be alleged, as except for the fish-days in summer they live almost exclusively on bananas and manioc.

That I should have to treat chronic nicotine poisoning out here I should never have believed. At first I could not tell what to think of acute constipation which was accompanied by nervous disturbances and only made worse by aperients, but while treating a black Government official who was suffering severely, I came to see clearly, through observation and questioning, that the misuse of tobacco lay at the root of it. The man soon got well and the case was much talked of, as he had been a sufferer for years and had become almost incapable of work. From that time, whenever a case of severe constipation came to me, I asked at once: "How many pipes a day do you smoke?," and I recognized in a few weeks what mischief nicotine produces here. It is among the women that cases of nicotine poisoning are most frequent. Joseph explained to me that the natives suffer much from insomnia, and then smoke all through the night in order to stupefy themselves.

Tobacco here...is frightfully common and also frightfully strong (much stronger than that which is smoked by white people), and it largely takes the place of small coins: e.g., one leaf, worth about a halfpenny, will buy two pineapples, and almost all temporary services are paid for by means of it. If you have to travel, you take for the purchase of food for the crew, not money, for that has no value in the forest, but a box of tobacco-leaves, and to prevent the men from helping themselves to its valuable contents you make it your seat. A pipe goes from mouth to mouth during the journey; and anybody who wants to travel fast and will promise his crew an extra two leaves each is sure to arrive an hour or two sooner than he otherwise would.

The teeth also give the natives much trouble. Many of my patients suffer from shrinking of the gums together with purulent discharges (*pyorrhoea*) caused by accumulations of tartar. Then, in the course of time, all the teeth get loose and fall out. Strange to say, these cases get well more quickly here than in Europe, where the complicated treatment often fails to attain its object. I have obtained successful results from regular painting with an alcoholic solution of thymol, only the patient has to be careful not to swallow any of the liquid, which is, of course, very poisonous.

It seems to the natives almost incredible that I can extract teeth which are not yet loose, but they do not all trust the polished forceps! A chief who was plagued with toothache would not submit to their use till he had gone home again to consult his wives. Presumably the family decision was unfavorable, as he did not present himself again. On the other hand, some request me to take all their teeth out and to get them new ones from Europe. A few old folk have, through the missionaries, actually got some double sets, "made by the white people," and they are now an object of much envy.

Abdominal tumors are very common here with the women. My hope that I should not need to perform any major operation before the medical ward was ready for use was disappointed. On August 15th I had to operate on a case of strangulated hernia which had been brought in the evening before. The man, whose name was Ainda, begged me to operate, for, like all natives, he knew well enough the dangers of his condition. There was, in fact, no time to lose, and the instruments were brought together as quickly as possible. Mr. Christol allowed me to use his boys' bedroom as an operating theater; my wife undertook to give the anesthetic, and a missionary acted as assistant. Everything went off better than we could have expected, but I was almost staggered by the quiet confidence with which the man placed himself in position on the operating table.

The aseptic precautions were, naturally, far from perfect, but the patient recovered....

Mental complaints are relatively rarer here than in Europe, though I have already seen some half-dozen such. They are a great worry as I do not know how to dispose of them. If they are allowed to remain on the station they disturb us with their cries all the night through, and I have to get up again and again to quieten them with a subcutaneous injection....

The condition of these poor creatures out here is dreadful. The natives do not know how to protect themselves from them. Confinement is impossible, as they can at any time break out of a bamboo hut. They are therefore bound with cords of bast, but that only makes their condition worse, and the final result almost always is that they are somehow or other got rid of....

[In one] case...an old man was brought with hands and feet bound. The ropes had cut deeply into his flesh, and hands and feet alike were covered with blood and sores. I was amazed at the small effect produced by the strongest doses of morphia, scopolamin, chloral hydrate, and bromide of potassium. On the second day Joseph said to me: "Doctor, believe me, the man is out of his mind because he has been poisoned. You will make nothing of him; he will get weaker and wilder, and at last he will die." And Joseph was right; in a fortnight the man was dead. From one of the Catholic fathers I learned that he had robbed some women and, therefore, had been followed up and poisoned by their relatives.

A similar case I was able to study from the beginning. One Sunday evening a woman arrived in a canoe writhing with cramp. I thought at first that it was simple hysteria, but the next day maniacal disturbance supervened, and during the night she began to rave and shriek. On her, too, the narcotics had hardly any effect, and her strength rapidly diminished. The natives surmised that she had been poisoned, and whether they were right or not I am not in a position to decide.

From all I hear it must be true that poison is much used in these parts, and farther south that is still oftener the case: the tribes between the Ogowe and the Congo are notorious in this respect. At the same time there are, among the natives, many inexplicable cases of sudden death which are quite unjustifiably regarded as the result of poison.

Anyhow, there must be many plants the juices of which have a peculiarly stimulating effect on the system. I have been assured by trustworthy persons that there are certain leaves and roots which enable men to row for a whole day without experiencing either hunger, thirst, or fatigue, and to display at the same time an increasingly boisterous merriment. I hope in time to learn something more definite about these "medicines," but it is always difficult to do so, because the knowledge about them is kept a strict secret. Anyone who is suspected of betraying anything about them, and above all if it is to a white man, may count with certainty on being poisoned.

That the medicine men employ poison to maintain their authority I learned in a peculiar way through Joseph. About the middle of the dry season his village went off to a sandbank about three hours upstream from here, on a fishing expedition. These fishing days are not unlike the Old Testament harvest festivals, when the people "rejoiced before Yahweh." Old and young live together for a fortnight in "booths" made with branches of trees, and at every meal eat fresh fish, boiled, baked, or stewed. Whatever is not consumed is dried and smoked, and if all goes well, a village may take home with it as many as ten thousand fish. As Joseph's eyes nearly start from their sockets whenever the conversation turns to fish, I proposed to allow him to go out with his village for the first afternoon and asked him to take a small tub in which to bring back a few fishes for the doctor. He showed, however, no enthusiasm at the prospect, and a few questions put me in possession of the reason. On the first day there is no fishing done, but the place is blessed. The "elders" pour rum and throw tobacco leaves into the water to put the evil spirits into a good humor, so that they may let the fish be caught in the nets and may injure no one. These ceremonies were once omitted several years ago, but the following year an old woman wrapped herself up in a net and let herself be drowned. "But why? Most of you are Christians!" I exclaimed; "you don't believe in these things!" "Certainly not," he replied, "but anyone who spoke against them or even allowed himself to smile while the rum and tobacco were being offered would assuredly be poisoned sooner or later. The medicine men never forgive, and they live among us without anyone knowing who they are." So he stayed at home the first day, but I allowed him to go some days later.

Besides the fear of poison there is also their dread of the supernatural power for evil which one man can exert over another, for the natives here believe that there are means of acquiring such powers. Whoever has the right fetish can do anything; he will always be successful when hunting, and he can bring bad luck, sickness, and death on anyone whom he wishes to injure. Europeans will never be able to understand how terrible is the life of the poor creatures who pass their days in continual fear of the fetishes which can be used against them. Only those who have seen this misery at close quarters will understand that it is a simple human duty to bring to these primitive peoples a new view of the world which can free them from these torturing superstitions. In this matter the greatest sceptic, did he find himself out here, would prove a real helper of mission work.

What is fetishism? It is something born of the fears of primitive man. Primitive man wants to possess some charm to protect him from the evil spirits in nature and from those of the dead, as well as from the power for evil of his fellow men, and this protecting power he attributes to certain objects which he carries about with him. He does not worship his fetish, but regards it as a little bit of property which cannot but be of service to him through its supernatural powers.

What makes a fetish? That which is unknown is supposed to have magical power. A fetish is composed of a number of little objects which fill a small bag, a buffalo horn, or a box; the things most commonly used are red feathers, small parcels of red earth, leopard's claws and teeth, and — bells from Europe! Bells of an old-fashioned shape which date from the barter transactions of the eighteenth century! Opposite the mission station an African has laid out a small cocoa plantation, and the fetish which is expected to protect it hangs on a tree in a corked bottle. Nowadays valuable fetishes are enclosed in tin boxes, so that they may not be damaged by termites, from whose ravages a wooden box gives no permanent protection.

There are big fetishes and little ones. A big one usually includes a piece of human skull, but it must be from the skull of someone who was killed expressly to provide the fetish. Last summer at a short distance below the station an elderly man was killed in a canoe. The murderer was discovered, and it is considered to have been proved that he committed the crime in order to secure the fetish by means of which he hoped to ensure the fulfillment of their contracts by people who owed him goods and money!...

I am myself the possessor of a fetish. The most important objects in it are two fragments of a human skull, of a longish oval shape and dyed with some sort of red coloring matter; they seem to me to be from the parietal bones. The owner was ill for many months, and his wife also, both suffering tortures from sleeplessness. Several times, however, the man heard in a dream a voice which revealed to him that they could get well only if they took the family fetish he had inherited to Mr. Haug, the missionary in N'Gomo, and followed Mr. Haug's orders. Mr. Haug referred him to me and made me a present of the fetish. The man and his wife stayed with me several weeks for treatment and were discharged with their health very much improved.

The belief that magical power dwells in human skulls which have been obtained expressly for this purpose must be a quite primitive one. I saw not long ago in a medical periodical the assertion that the supposed cases of trephining which have often been recognized during the excavation and examination of prehistoric graves were by no means attempts at treatment of tumors on the brain or similar growths, as had been assumed, but were simply operations for the securing of fetish objects. The author of the article is probably right.

— *On the Edge of the Primeval Forest*

A Hernia Operation

As to operations...the one I have had to perform oftenest is that for hernia, a thing which afflicts the Africans of Central Africa much more than it does white people, though why this should be so we do not know. They also suffer much oftener than white people from strangulated hernia, in which the intestine becomes constricted and blocked, so that it can no longer empty itself. It then becomes enormously inflated by the gases which form, and this causes terrible pain. Then after several days of torture, death takes place, unless the intestine can be got back through the rupture into the abdomen. Our ancestors were well acquainted with this terrible method of dying, but we no longer see it in Europe because every case is operated upon as soon as ever it is recognized.... But in Africa this terrible death is quite common. There are few Africans who have not as boys seen some man rolling in the sand of his hut and howling with agony till death came to release him. So now, the moment a man feels that his rupture is a strangulated one — rupture is far rarer among women — he begs his friends to put him in a canoe and bring him to me.

How can I describe my feelings when a poor fellow is brought me in this condition? I am the only person within hundreds of miles who can help him. Because I am here and am supplied by my friends with the necessary means, he can be saved, like those who came before him in the same condition and those who will come after him, while otherwise he would have fallen a victim to the torture. This does not mean merely that I can save his life. We must all die. But that I can save him from days of torture, that is what I feel as my great and ever new privilege. Pain is a more terrible lord of mankind than even death himself.

So, when the poor, moaning creature comes, I lay my hand on his forehead and say to him: "Don't be afraid! In an hour's time you shall be put to sleep, and when you wake you won't feel any more pain." Very soon he is given an injection of omnipon; the doctor's wife is called to the hospital, and, with Joseph's help, makes everything ready for the operation. When that is to begin she administers the anesthetic, and Joseph, in a long pair of rubber gloves, acts as assistant.

The operation is finished, and in the hardly lighted dormitory, I watch for the sick man's awaking. Scarcely has he

recovered consciousness when he stares about him and ejac-
ulates again and again: "I've no more pain! I've no more
pain!..." His hand feels for mine and will not let it go. Then
I begin to tell him and the others who are in the room that it
is the Lord Jesus who has told the doctor and his wife to come
to the Ogowe, and that white people in Europe give them the
money to live here and cure the sick Africans. Then I have to
answer questions as to who these white people are, where they
live, and how they know that the natives suffer so much from
sickness. The African sun is shining through the coffee bushes
into the dark shed, but we, black and white, sit side by side
and feel that we know by experience the meaning of the words:
"And all ye are brethren" (Matt. xxiii. 8). Would that my gen-
erous friends in Europe could come out here and live through
one such hour!   — On the Edge of the Primeval Forest

Moral Problems in Africa

*The charge of paternalism has always been brought against
Schweitzer by those who have had none of the experiences he
had. To this one can only point out that he grew up with ro-
mantic notions of the Noble Savage in his mind, and the reality
came as a great shock. To do his job properly he had to face
facts, but in so doing he always sought to understand the context in which both Africans and whites existed and the various
physical and social pressures that determined their behavior. In
such a situation the word "paternalist" is simply facile.*

A white man can have real authority only if the native respects
him. No one must imagine that the child of nature looks up
to us merely because we know more, or can do more than he
can. This superiority is so obvious to him that it ceases to be
taken into account. It is by no means the case that the white
man is to the African an imposing person because he possesses
railway and steamers, can fly in the air, or travel under water.

"White people are clever and can do anything they want to," says Joseph. The African is not in a position to estimate what these technical conquests of nature mean as proofs of mental and spiritual superiority, but on one point he has an unerring intuition, and that is on the question whether any particular white man is a real, moral personality or not. If the native feels that he is this, moral authority is possible; if not, it is simply impossible to create it. The child of nature, not having been artificialized and spoiled as we have been, has only elementary standards of judgment, and he measures us by the most elementary of them all, the moral standard. Where he finds goodness, justice, and genuineness of character, real worth and dignity, that is, behind the external dignity given by social circumstances, he bows and acknowledges his master; where he does not find them he remains really defiant in spite of all appearance of submission and says to himself: "This white man is no more of a man than I am, for he is not a better one than I am."

I am not thinking merely of the fact that many unsuitable and not a few quite unworthy men go out into the colonies of all nations. I wish to emphasize a further fact that even the morally best and the idealists find it difficult out here to be what they wish to be. We all get exhausted in the terrible contest between the European worker who bears the responsibility and is always in a hurry, and the child of nature who does not know what responsibility is and is never in a hurry. The Government official has to record at the end of the year so much work done by the natives in building and road maintenance, in service as carrier or boatman, and so much money paid in taxes; the trader and the planter are expected by their companies to provide so much profit for the capital invested in the enterprise. But in all this they are forever dependent on men who cannot share the responsibility that weighs on them, who only give just so much return of labor as the others can force out of them, and who, if there is the slightest failure in superintendence, do exactly as they like without any regard for the loss that may be caused to

their employers. In this daily and hourly contest with the child
of nature every white man is continually in danger of gradual
moral ruin....

Not long ago the termites, or white ants, got into a box
which stood on our veranda. I emptied the box and broke it up,
and gave the pieces to the African who had been helping me.
"Look," I said to him, "the ants have got into it; you mustn't
put the wood with the rest of the firewood or the ants will get
into the framework of the hospital building. Go down to the
river and throw it into the water. Do you understand?"

"Yes, yes, you need not worry." It was late in the day and,
being too tired to go down the hill again, I was inclined to break
my general rule and trust an African — one who was in fact on
the whole intelligent and handy. But about ten o'clock I felt so
uneasy that I took the lantern and went down to the hospital.
There was the wood with the ants in it lying with the rest of the
firewood. To save himself the trouble of going the twenty yards
down to the river, the African had endangered all my buildings!

The greater the responsibility that rests on a white man, the
greater the danger of his becoming hard towards the natives.
We on a mission staff are too easily inclined to become self-
righteous with regard to the other whites. We have not got to
obtain such and such results from the natives by the end of the
year, as officials and traders have, and therefore this exhausting
contest is not so hard a one for us as for them. I no longer venture to judge my fellows after learning something of the soul
of the white man who is in business from those who lay as
patients under my roof, and whose talk has led me to suspect
that those who now speak savagely about the natives may have
come out to Africa full of idealism, but in the daily contest have
become weary and hopeless, losing little by little what they once
possessed of spirituality.

That it is so hard to keep oneself really humane, and so to
be a standard bearer of civilization, that is the tragic element in

the problem of the relations between white and colored men in Equatorial Africa.   — *On the Edge of the Primeval Forest*

A Sermon at Lambaréné

I try to be as concrete as possible. No vague generalizations to explain, for example, Peter's question to Jesus: "How many times should I forgive my brother? Should it be seven times?" (Matthew 18:21). I talk to my people with complete realism, and I use everyday incidents to illustrate the meaning of forgiving seven times in a single day. This is how I recently tackled it:

"One morning, you have just got up, and you leave your hut. Coming towards you you see a man whom everybody thinks is a scoundrel. He does you an injury. You remember that Jesus has said that one should forgive; you keep quiet instead of starting an argument.

"Next your neighbor's goat eats the bananas you were keeping for your dinner. Instead of seeking a quarrel with him, you merely tell him what his goat has done and that it would he fair if he replaced your bananas. But if he contests this and pretends that it wasn't his goat, you go on your way peacefully and you reflect that the Almighty has provided so many bananas on your plantation that it's not worth the trouble of starting a fight over the odd bunch.... "

[*After another four misadventures evening comes and —*]

"You want to go fishing but you discover that your canoe has disappeared. Someone has gone off in it to do his own fishing. Angrily you hide yourself behind a tree to await him, and you promise yourself that when he gets back you'll seize his fish, you'll make a complaint against him and make him pay a fair compensation. But while you lie in wait, your heart starts to speak. It keeps repeating to you the words of Jesus: 'God cannot forgive us our sins if we do not forgive each others'.' You have to wait so long that the Lord Jesus once more wins the victory. When the other fellow comes back at the crack of dawn and stands all confused when he sees you step out from behind your tree, you don't start punching him, but tell him that the Lord Jesus forces you to forgive him; and you let him go. You do not even claim the fish which he has caught, unless he offers them of his own accord. But I think that he will give them to you, from sheer amazement that you haven't made a fuss.

"Then you go home, happy and proud that you have succeeded in forgiving seven times. But suppose that very day the Lord Jesus comes into your village; you introduce yourself to him, imagining that he will praise you before all the world for your good deeds. Not at all. He will tell you, as he told Peter, that seven times is still not enough — that one must forgive yet another seven times, and yet again, and a fourth time's seven times and plenty more times, if you also want God always to forgive you."   — "Un culte du dimanche en forêt vierge"

War, and the Genesis of Reverence for Life

My wife and I had completed our second dry season in Africa and were beginning to sketch out plans for going home at the opening of the third, when on August 5, 1914, the news came that war had broken out in Europe. On the evening of that very day we were informed that we must consider ourselves to be prisoners of war; we might, indeed, for the present remain in our own house, but we must stop all intercourse with either white people or natives, and obey unconditionally the regulations of the black soldiers who were assigned us as guards. One of the missionaries and his wife, who like ourselves were Alsatians, were also interned at the Lambaréné mission station. The only thing about the war which the natives understood at first was that it was all over with the timber trade, and that all commodities had become dearer. It was only later, when many of them were transported to Cameroon to serve as carriers for the active forces, that they began to understand what the war really meant.

As soon as it became known that of the white men who used to live on the Ogowe ten had already fallen, an old African remarked "What, so many men killed already in this war! Why don't their tribes meet to talk out the palaver? How can they ever pay for all these dead men?" For in native warfare those who fall, whether among the conquerors or the conquered, have to be paid for by the opposite side. This same African expressed the criticism that Europeans kill each other merely out of cruelty, because of course they don't want to eat the dead....

When I was forbidden to work in the hospital, I thought at first that I would proceed to the completion of my book on St. Paul. But another subject at once forced itself upon me, one which I had had in my mind for years, and which the war was now making a real live issue: the problem of our civilization. So on the second day of my internment, still quite amazed at being able to sit down at my writing table early in the morning as in the days before I took up medicine, I set to work on the *Philosophy of Civilization.* ...

At the beginning of the summer of 1915 I awoke from a sort of stupor. Why only criticism of civilization? ... Why not go on to something constructive?

So now I began a search for the knowledge and convictions to which we must refer the will to civilization and the power to realize it....

Before long Schweitzer was allowed to resume his medical work. Sick Africans took a poor view of the cocky young African soldiers who were ordering their respected doctor about. And besides, some of them were sick too. The military relented. But the thoughts about civilization went on.

As I worked I became clear about the connection between civilization and worldview (*Weltanschauung*), and I recognized that the catastrophe of civilization started from a catastrophe of worldview.

The ideals of true civilization had become powerless, because the idealistic worldview in which they are rooted has been gradually lost to us. All the happenings which come about within nations and within mankind as a whole arise out of spiritual causes which are contained in the prevailing worldview.

But what is civilization?

We may take as the essential element in civilization the ethical perfecting of the individual and of society as well. But at the same time, every spiritual and every material step in advancement has a significance for civilization. The will to civilization is then the universal will to progress which is conscious of the ethical as the highest value for all. In spite of the great importance we attach to the triumphs of knowledge and achievement, it is nevertheless obvious that only a humanity which is striving after ethical ends can in full measure share in the blessings brought by material progress and become master of the dangers which accompany it. To the generation which had adopted a belief in an immanent power of progress realizing itself in some measure naturally and automatically, and which thought that it no longer needed any ethical ideals but could advance to its goal by means of knowledge and achievement alone, terrible proof was being given by its present position of the error into which it had sunk.

The only possible way out of the present chaos is for us to adopt a worldview which will bring us once more under the control of the ideals of true civilization which are contained in it.

Even we Europeans have only in the course of time and through a change in our worldview arrived at our will to progress. In antiquity and in the Middle Ages there was nothing more than attempts at it. Greek thinking does try to reach a worldview of world- and life-affirmation, but it fails in the attempt and ends in resignation. The worldview of the Middle Ages is determined by the ideas of primitive Christianity as brought into harmony with Greek metaphysics. It is fundamentally world- and life-negating because the interest of that stage of Christianity was concentrated on a super-sensible world. All that in the Middle Ages made itself felt as world- and life-affirmation is a fruit of the active ethic contained in the preaching of Jesus and of the creative forces of the fresh and unspoiled new peoples on whom Christianity had imposed a worldview which was in contradiction to their nature.

Then little by little the world- and life-affirmation that was already germinating among the peoples formed as a result of the *Volkerwanderung* (the Great Migration) begins to manifest itself. The Renaissance proclaims its rejection of the world- and life-negating worldview of the Middle Ages. And an ethical character is given to this new world- and life-affirmation by its taking over from Christianity the ethic of love taught by Jesus. This, as an ethic of activity, is strong enough to throw off the worldview of life- and world-negation in which it arose, to unite itself with the new world- and life-affirmation, and thereby to reach the ideal of realizing a spiritual and ethical world within the natural world.

The striving for material and spiritual progress, then, which characterizes the peoples of modern Europe, has its source in the worldview to which these peoples have come. As a result of the Renaissance and the spiritual and religious movements bound up with it, men have entered on a new relation to themselves and to the world, and this has aroused in them a need to create by their own activities spiritual and material values which shall help to a higher development of individuals and of mankind. It is not the case that the man of modern Europe is enthusiastic for progress because he may hope to get some personal advantage from it. He is less concerned about his own condition than about the happiness which he hopes will be the lot of coming generations. Enthusiasm for progress has taken possession of him. Impressed by his great experience of finding the world revealed to him as constituted and maintained by forces which carry out a definite design, he himself wills to become an active, purposeful force in the world. He looks with confidence towards new and better times which shall dawn for mankind, and learns by experience that the ideals which are held and acted upon by the mass of people do win power over circumstances and remold them.

It is on his will to material progress, acting in union with the will to ethical progress, that the foundations of modern civilization are being laid....

In modern European thought there is being enacted a tragedy, in that by a slow but irresistible process the bonds originally existing between world- and-life-affirmation and the ethical are becoming slack and are finally being severed. The result that we are coming to is that European humanity is being guided by a will-to-progress that has become merely external and has lost its bearings.

World- and life-affirmation can produce of itself only a partial and imperfect civilization. Only if it becomes inward and ethical can the will-to-progress which results from it possess the requisite insight to distinguish the valuable from the less valuable, and strive after a civilization which does not consist only in achievements of knowledge and power, but before all else will make men, both individually and collectively, more spiritual and more ethical.

But how could it come about that the modern worldview of world- and life-affirmation, ethical as it was originally, changed and became non-ethical?

The only possible explanation is that it was not really founded on thought. The thought out of which it arose was noble and enthusiastic but not deep. The intimate connection of the ethical with world- and life-affirmation was for it a matter of feeling and experience rather than of proof. It took the side of world-

and life-affirmation and of the ethical, without having penetrated their inner nature and their inward connection.

This noble and valuable worldview, then, being rooted in belief rather than in thought which penetrated to the real nature of things, was bound to wither and lose its power over the minds of men. All subsequent thinking about the problems of ethics and of the relation of man to his world could not but expose the weak points in this worldview, and thereby help to hasten its decay. Its activity took effect in this direction even when its intention was to give support, for it never succeeded in replacing the inadequate foundation by one that was adequate. Again and again the new foundations and the underpinning masonry which it had taken in hand showed themselves too weak to support the building.

Thanks to my apparently abstract, yet absolutely practical thinking about the connection of civilization with worldview, I had come to see the decay of civilization as a result of a growing impotence in the traditional modern worldview of ethical world- and life-affirmation, an impotence which there was no arresting. It had become clear to me that, like so many other people, I had clung to that worldview from inner necessity, without troubling at all about how far it could really be proved by thought.

I had got so far during the summer of 1915. But what was to come next?

Was the difficulty soluble which till now had seemed insoluble? Or had we to regard the worldview through which alone civilization is possible as an illusion within us which never ceases to stir our hearts yet never really gets dominion over us? To continue holding it up to our generation as something to be believed seemed to me foolish and hopeless. Only if it offers itself to us as something desired from the depth of thought can it become spiritually our own.

At bottom I remained convinced that the mutual connection between world- and life-affirmation and the ethical, declared to belong to that worldview which it had been found hitherto impossible to carry out fully, had come from a presentiment of the truth. So it was necessary to undertake to grasp as a necessity of thought by fresh, simple, and sincere thinking the truth which had hitherto been only suspected and believed in although so often proclaimed as proved.

In undertaking this I seemed to myself to be like a man who has to build a new and better boat to replace a rotten one in which he can no longer venture to trust himself to the sea, and yet does not know how to begin.

For months on end I lived in a continual state of mental excitement. Without the least success I let my thought be concentrated, even all through my daily work at the hospital, on the real nature of world- and life-affirmation and of ethics, and on the question of what they have in common. I was wandering about in a thicket in which no path was to be found. I was leaning with all my might against an iron door which would not yield.

All that I had learned from philosophy about ethics left me in the lurch. The conceptions of the Good which it had offered were all so lifeless, so unelemental, so narrow, and so destitute of content that it was quite impossible to bring them into union with world- and life-affirmation. Moreover philosophy could be said never to have concerned itself with the problem of the connection between civilization and worldview. The modern world- and life-affirmation had become to it such a matter of course that it had felt no need for coming to clear ideas about it.

To my surprise I had also to establish the fact that the central province of philosophy, into which meditation about civilization and worldview had led me, was practically unexplored land. Now from this point, now from that, I tried to penetrate to its interior, but again and again I had to give up the attempt. I was already exhausted and disheartened. I saw, indeed, the conception needed before me, but I could not grasp it and give it expression.

While in this mental condition I had to undertake a longish journey on the river. I was staying with my wife on the coast at Cape Lopez for the sake of her health — it was in September 1915 — when I was summoned to visit Madame Pelot, the ailing wife of a missionary, at N'Gomo, about 160 miles upstream. The only means of conveyance I could find was a small steamer, towing an overladen barge, which was on the point of starting. Except myself, there were only natives on board, but among them was Emil Ogouma, my friend from Lambaréné. Since I had been in too much of a hurry to provide myself with enough food for the journey, they let me share the contents of their cooking pot. Slowly we crept upstream, laboriously feeling — it was the dry season — for the channels between the sandbanks. Lost in thought I sat on the deck of the barge, struggling to find the elementary and universal conception of the ethical which I had not discovered in any philosophy. Sheet after sheet I covered with disconnected sentences, merely to keep myself concentrated on the problem. Late on the third day, at the very moment when, at sunset, we were making our way through a herd of hippopotamuses, there flashed upon my mind, unforeseen and unsought, the phrase, "Reverence for Life." The iron door had yielded: the path in the thicket had become visible. Now I had found my way to the idea in which world- and life-affirmation and ethics are contained side by side! Now I knew that the worldview of ethical world- and life-affirmation, together with its ideals of civilization, is founded in thought.

— *My Life and Thought*

4

Reverence for Life

From the moment when Schweitzer hit upon the phrase "Reverence for Life" — or rather from the moment when it first hit him — it dominated both his thought and his life. The haunting passion for nature which he had felt since childhood fused with his desperate quest for the foundation of human ethics, and the vision was born. Everything led to life itself, everything stemmed from it. Good is what promotes and preserves life. Evil is what destroys and injures life. That is enough.

Schweitzer approached the subject at many times of his life and from many angles — the philosophical, the inspirational, the analytical, and the personal, each reinforcing and amplifying the others. Readers who find the subject attractive but who yet have questions, can, I believe, find all the answers in Civilization and Ethics, *chapter 17, and in the epilogue that he wrote in 1931 for his major autobiographical work,* My Life and Thought. *But though he himself fought so hard to find an intellectual foundation for this great ethical conception, he knew very well that it is in the heart, not the head, that the world must respond to it, if it responds at all. It was in his heart from a very early age.*

AN INSTINCT FOR NATURE

Childhood Feeling for Animal Life

As far back as I can remember I was saddened by the amount of misery I saw in the world around me. Youth's unqualified joie de vivre I never really knew, and I believe that to be the case with many children, even though they appear outwardly merry and quite free from care.

One thing that specially saddened me was that the unfortunate animals had to suffer so much pain and misery. The sight of an old limping horse, tugged forward by one man while another kept beating it with a stick to get it to the knacker's yard at Colmar, haunted me for weeks.

It was quite incomprehensible to me — this was before I began going to school — why in my evening prayers I should pray for human beings only. So when my mother had prayed with me and had kissed me good-night, I used to add silently a prayer that I had composed myself for all living creatures. It ran thus: "O heavenly Father, protect and bless all things that have breath; guard them from all evil, and let them sleep in peace...."

A deep impression was made on me by something which happened during my seventh or eighth year. Henry Brasch and I had made catapults for ourselves out of strips of india-rubber, with which we could shoot small stones. It was spring and the end of Lent, when one morning Henry said to me, "Come along, let's go on to the Rebberg and shoot some birds." This was to me a terrible proposal, but I did not venture to refuse for fear he should laugh at me. We got close to a tree which was still without any leaves, and on which the birds were singing beautifully to greet the morning, without showing the least fear of us. Then stooping like a Red Indian hunter, my companion put a bullet in the leather of his catapult and took aim. In obedience to his nod of command, I did the same, though with

terrible twinges of conscience, vowing to myself that I would
shoot the moment that he did. At that very moment the church
bells began to ring, mingling their music with the songs of the
birds and the sunshine. It was the Warning-bell, which began
half an hour before the regular peal-ringing, and for me it was
a voice from heaven. I shooed the birds away, so that they flew
where they were safe from my companion's catapult, and then I
fled home. And ever since then, when the Passiontide bells ring
out to the leafless trees and the sunshine, I reflect with a rush of
grateful emotion how on that day their music drove deep into
my heart the commandment: "Thou shalt not kill."

From that day onward I took courage to emancipate myself from the fear of men, and whenever my inner convictions
were at stake I let other people's opinions weigh less with me
than they had done previously. I tried also to unlearn my former dread of being laughed at by my school fellows. This early
influence upon me of the commandment not to kill or to torture other creatures is the great experience of my childhood and
youth. By the side of that all others are insignificant.

While I was still going to the village school we had a dog
with a light brown coat, named Phylax. Like many others of his
kind, he could not endure a uniform, and always went for the
postman. I was, therefore, commissioned to keep him in order
whenever the postman came, for he was inclined to bite, and
had already been guilty of the crime of attacking a policeman.
So I used to take a switch and drive him into a corner of the
yard, and keep him there till the postman had gone. What a
feeling of pride it gave to me to stand, like a wild beast tamer,
before him while he barked and showed his teeth, and to control him with blows of the switch whenever he tried to break
out of the corner! But this feeling of pride did not last. When,
later in the day, we sat side by side as friends, I blamed myself
for having struck him; I knew that I could keep him back from
the postman if I held him by his collar and stroked him. But

when the fatal hour came round again I yielded once more to the pleasurable intoxication of being a wild beast tamer!

During the holidays I was allowed to act as driver for our next-door neighbor. His chestnut horse was old and asthmatic, and was not allowed to trot much, but in my pride of driver-ship I let myself again and again be seduced into whipping him into a trot, even though I knew and felt that he was tired. The pride of sitting behind a trotting horse infatuated me, and the man let me go on in order not to spoil my pleasure. But what was the end of the pleasure? When we got home and I noticed during the unharnessing what I had not looked at in the same way when I was in the cart, viz. how the poor animal's flanks were working, what good was it to me to look into his tired eyes and silently ask him to forgive me?

On another occasion — it was while I was at the Gymnasium, and at home for the Christmas holidays I was driving a sledge when neighbor Loscher's dog, which was known to be vicious, ran yelping out of the house and sprang at the horse's head. I thought I was fully justified in trying to sting him up well with the whip, although it was evident that he only ran at the sledge in play. But my aim was too good; the lash caught him in the eye, and he rolled howling in the snow. His cries of pain haunted me; I could not get them out of my ears for weeks. I have twice gone fishing with rod and line just because other boys asked me to, but this sport was soon made impossible for me by the treatment of the worms that were put on the hook for bait, and the wrenching of the mouths of the fishes that were caught. I gave it up, and even found courage enough to dissuade other boys from going.

From experiences like these, which moved my heart and often made me feel ashamed, there slowly grew up in me an unshakeable conviction that we have no right to inflict suffering and death on another living creature unless there is some unavoidable necessity for it, and that we ought all of us to feel what a horrible thing it is to cause suffering and death out of mere thoughtlessness. And this conviction has influenced me only more and more strongly with time. I have grown more and more certain that at the bottom of our hearts we all think this, and that we fail to acknowledge it and to carry our belief into practice chiefly because we are afraid of being laughed at by other people as sentimentalists, though partly also because we allow our best feelings to get blunted. But I vowed that I would never let my feelings get blunted, and that I would never be afraid of the reproach of sentimentalism.

I never go to a menagerie because I cannot endure the sight of the misery of the captive animals. The exhibiting of trained animals I abhor. What an amount of suffering and cruel punishment the poor creatures have to endure in order to give a few moments' pleasure to men devoid of all thought and feeling for them!   — *Memoirs of Childhood and Youth*

Mystical Union with Nature

The cows graze in the dark green fields. A blue mist hovers above. Everything looks subdued; the mountains are shrouded, out of this blue, translucent sea you can hear the sound of the cowbells, from far and near, unreal in its rhythm and harmony — I feel like reading in a storybook — a red ladybug runs over my paper. — The brown blades of grass and last little flowers shiver in the wind. — could I only capture this last hour of peaceful Fall....

Is it strength or weakness to live in such a mystical union with nature, to feel the effects of its smile and its tears deeply in one's soul... ?   — Letter to Hélène, November 9, 1902

My rock lies above the valley — a small wilderness surrounded by vines: honeysuckle and blackberries fight for first place; blue sloes and red rose-hips tell about the beauty of last spring. Now the modest fall flowers are still in bloom, and dry grass blades shiver in the east wind. Everything is enveloped in a blue, gossamer veil out of which the distant mountain chain shows like a silhouette. In the meadows they mow and the fragrance of the hay invigorates the air up here. Late butterflies look for fluttering companions; on the bare fields trees appear in harsh outlines, as if they painted the skeletons of bodies that are still filled with lush vitality. But I see everything in its splendor.

Now, however, I have to turn to my work, although I would love to dream in this invigorating fall atmosphere.

—Letter to Hélène, September 8, 1902

Now nature gives in. Two days it fought and wrestled against its ageing. Rain and storm, wild clouds that raced gloomily in the sky accompany the wild pain with which the soul of nature rises up so passionately — An overnight peace has come. Nature now smiles in bright sunshine, like someone who has overcome and the raindrops shine in the grape leaves like tears of past sorrows. Now the faded flowers and bare meadows do not hurt anymore. Shiny rose-hips and dark sloes decorate nature as if it were blossoming again. It puts brilliant jewelry on its dark and serious robe.   —Letter to Hélène, September 12, 1902

THE DEVELOPMENT OF AN IDEA

The generation following the 1914–18 war is generally held responsible for the beginning of the end of the old values. Not so, according to Schweitzer. He had felt it in the air years before.

He had reached the conclusion that a specific mental conflict had crippled the image which Europeans had traditionally held of the world they lived in. Briefly, the argument runs thus: Europeans in general believe that life is worth living. They have, that is to say, a positive approach to life on this earth. The endeavor of European philosophers has been to prove that this positive approach to life is justified by the fact that the universe

*itself is beneficent — that goodness, or love, is part of the na-
ture of things. This connection Schweitzer called "world- and
life-affirmation." Many splendid theories have been evolved to
demonstrate the excellence of the universe, and they all had two
things in common: that their ideals were admirable; and that
they had the practical advantage of confirming people in general in their trust in divine providence (or whatever it might be
called).*

*But each theory in turn proved vulnerable to criticism. And
when finally in the nineteenth century the study of natural science began to be taken seriously and people began to look for
truth not in academic theories but in physical observation and
experiments, it soon became clear that there is really nothing
at all in nature that one can truly call loving. Nature is an in-
different force, creating and destroying impartially. For every
sign of kindliness there is an opposing cruelty. The idealistic pictures drawn by philosophers, clerics, and moralists were simply
wish-fulfilling figments of the imagination.*

*Since European morality had always depended on this sup-
posed universal pattern (the human mind being seen in some
way as the mirror of the universal mind), the shattering of
the pattern left morality without any basis. Since human beings could find nothing in nature on which to peg their ideals,
they were free (this was never quite stated but was implied) to
become as amoral as nature.*

*Such, put crudely, was Schweitzer's "apparently abstract,
yet absolutely practical thinking about the connection between
civilization and worldview." It led to his search for the anti-
dote to Europe's sickness. Somewhere, Schweitzer felt, some
basic principle of civilization had been missed, or mislaid — a
principle that would underwrite the validity of human ideals,
proving that love was not simply a sentimental invention or a
convenient way of holding society together.*

*Then came the mental turmoil out of which came the revela-
tion of Reverence for Life.*

Reverence for Life is a translation of the German Ehrfurcht vor dem Leben, *and the word "reverence" is really not quite adequate. It lacks the German word's overtones of awe before an overwhelming force.* Ehrfurcht *is respect carried to ultimate lengths. It holds reverberations of the feelings we experience on the tops of high mountains, in a storm at sea, or in a tropical tornado. This was the element that the African jungle gave to Schweitzer's thinking — the acknowledgment of immensity and of overwhelming power, the force of continuing life and ever-present death in the vastness of nature, carrying with it an unavoidable sense of moral responsibility toward life in all its forms.*

This is a poetic concept. It came to him after much diligent thought, true, but it came out of the blue, an intuition, not a logical answer to an intellectual problem. So how can he call it a product of thought, or worse still, a necessity of thought?

Many readers of Schweitzer have been troubled by this problem and have criticized him for failing to notice that Reverence for Life is not a necessity of thought, that no logical sequence of propositions compels anyone to arrive at Reverence for Life. It is simply Schweitzer's own personal view of life summed up in a phrase, and thought has nothing to do with it.

But Schweitzer's word "denken" carries other connotations, of meditation, of brooding absorption in a subject, which the word "thought" does not encompass. For example, in The Decay and Restoration of Civilization, *this is how he defines it: "thought is no dry intellectualism, which would suppress all the manifold movements of our inner life, but the totality of all the functions of our spirit in their living action and interaction." And in his Hibbert lectures in 1934: "Thinking is a harmony within us."*

Perhaps the clearest statement of his attitude and the way he reached it comes from a statement he made in an interview on Radio Brazzaville in 1953:

I was always, even as a boy, engrossed in the philosophical problem of the relation between emotion and reason. Certain truths originate in feeling, others in the mind. Those truths that we derive from our emotions are of a moral kind — compassion, kindness, forgiveness, love for our neighbor. Reason, on the other hand, teaches us the truths that come from reflection.

But with the great spirits of our world — the Hebrew prophets, Christ, Zoroaster, the Buddha, and others — feeling is always paramount. In them emotion holds its ground against reason, and all of us have an inner assurance that the truth of emotion that these great spiritual figures reveal to us is the most profound and the most important truth.

The problem presented itself to me in these terms: must we really be condemned to live in this dualism of emotional and rational truths? Since my particular preoccupation was with problems of morality, I have always been struck by finding myself forced to recognize that the morality elaborated by philosophy, both ancient and modern, has been meager indeed when compared to the morality of the great religious and ethical geniuses who have taught us that the supreme and only truth capable of satisfying man's spirit is love.

I reached a point where I asked myself this question: does the mind, in its striving for a morality that can guide us in life, lag so far behind the morality that emotion reveals because it is not sufficiently profound to be able to conceive what the great teachers, in obedience to feeling, have made known to us?

This led me to devote myself entirely to the search for a fundamental principle of morality. Others before me have done the same. Throughout history there have been philosophers who believed intuitively that reason must eventually succeed in discovering the true and profound nature of the good. I have tried to carry their work further. In so doing, I was brought to the point where I had to consider the question of what the fundamental idea of existence is. What is the mind's point of departure when it sets itself the task of reflecting on humanity and on the world in which we live? This point of departure, I said to myself, is not any knowledge of the world that we have acquired. We do not have — and we will never have — true knowledge of the world; such knowledge will always remain a mystery to us.

The point of departure naturally offered for meditation between ourselves and the world is the simple evidence that we are life that wishes to live and are animated by a will in the midst of other lives animated by the same will. Simply by considering the act of thinking, our consciousness tells us this. True knowledge of the world consists in our being penetrated by a sense of the mystery of existence and of life.

•

If rational thought thinks itself out to a conclusion, it arrives at something non-rational which, nevertheless, is a necessity of thought. This is the paradox which dominates our spiritual life. If we try to get on without this non-rational element, there result views of the world and of life which have neither vitality nor value.

All valuable conviction is non-rational and has an emotional character, because it cannot be derived from knowledge of the world but arises out of the thinking experience of our will-to-live, in which we stride out beyond all knowledge of the world. This fact it is which the rational thought that thinks itself out to a conclusion comprehends as the truth by which we must live. The way to true mysticism leads up through rational thought to deep experience of the world and of our will-to-live. We must all venture once more to be "thinkers," so as to reach mysticism, which is the only direct and the only profound worldview. We must all wander in the field of knowledge to the point where knowledge passes over into experience of the world. We must all, through thought, become religious.

— Radio Brazzaville interview, 1953, quoted in Anderson, *The Schweitzer Album*

When the conception of the universal is reached and a man reflects upon his relation to the totality of being and to Being in itself, the resultant mysticism becomes widened, deepened, and purified. The entrance into the super-earthly and eternal then takes place through an act of thinking.

In this act the conscious personality raises itself above that illusion of the senses which makes him regard himself as in bondage in the present life to the earthly and temporal. It attains the power to distinguish between appearance and reality and is able to conceive the material as a mode of manifestation of the Spiritual. It has sight of the Eternal in the Transient. Recognizing the unity of all things in God, in Being as such, it passes beyond the unquiet flux of becoming and disintegration into the peace of timeless being, and is conscious of itself as being in God, and in every moment eternal.

This intellectual mysticism is a common possession of humanity. Whenever thought makes the ultimate effort to conceive the relation of the personality to the universal, this mysticism comes into existence.   — *The Mysticism of Paul the Apostle*

As in my will-to-live there is ardent desire for further life, and for the mysterious exaltation of the will-to-live which we call pleasure, while there is fear of destruction and of that mysterious depreciation of the will-to-live which we call pain: so too are these in the will-to-live around me, whether it can express itself to me, or remains dumb....

The man who has become a thinking being feels a compulsion to give to every will-to-live the same reverence for life that he gives to his own. He experiences that other life in his own. He accepts as being good: to preserve life, to promote life, to raise to its highest value life which is capable of development; and as being evil: to destroy life, to injure life, to repress life which is capable of development. This is the absolute, fundamental principle of the moral, and it is a necessity of thought.

The great fault of all ethics hitherto has been that they be-lieved themselves to have to deal only with the relations of man to man. In reality, however, the question is what is his attitude to the world and all life that comes within his reach. A man is ethical only when life, as such, is sacred to him, that of plants and animals as that of his fellow-men, and when he devotes himself helpfully to all life that is in need of help. Only the uni-versal ethic of the feeling of responsibility in an ever-widening sphere for all that lives — only that ethic can be founded in thought. The ethic of the relation of man to man is not some-thing apart by itself: it is only a particular relation which results from the universal one.

The ethic of Reverence for Life, therefore, comprehends within itself everything that can be described as love, devotion, and sympathy whether in suffering, joy, or effort.

The world, however, offers us the horrible drama of will-to-live divided against itself. One existence holds its own at the cost of another: one destroys another. Only in the thinking man has the will-to-live become conscious of other will-to-live, and desirous of solidarity with it. This solidarity, however, he cannot completely bring about, because man is subject to the puzzling and horrible law of being obliged to live at the cost of other life, and to incur again and again the guilt of destroy-ing and injuring life. But as an ethical being he strives to escape whenever possible from this necessity, and as one who has be-come enlightened and merciful to put a stop to this disunion (*Selbstentzweiung*) of the will-to-live so far as the influence of his own existence reaches. He thirsts to be permitted to pre-serve his humanity and to be able to bring to other existences release from their sufferings.   — *My Life and Thought*

Reverence for Life was a vision, an inspiration. It came upon Schweitzer as Peer Gynt came upon Ibsen or the theory of rel-ativity came upon Einstein. Ibsen had to write the play and make it work. Einstein had to find the mathematical proofs.

And Schweitzer had first to check his vision against the theories of other philosophers, and then, because he was talking about life, he had to make his life his argument.

The final chapters of Civilization and Ethics *should be read by anyone curious to know what living his argument felt like to a man doing it, for they are the fullest and most exhilarating exposition of Reverence for Life that he ever wrote, a paean of delight in the new possibilities of living.*

•

To recapitulate a little: the belief in goodness and gentleness had so long and so completely depended on a belief in the Divine Pattern that it was unthinkable that the two could be separated. Schweitzer separated them. In his own eyes he seemed extremely daring. Long chapters are devoted to the novelty of the claim that one could be agnostic about the design of the universe and still find significance and the foundation of ethics in mankind — that worldview could be dissociated from life view.

To understand the meaning of the whole — and that is what a worldview demands — is for us an impossibility.... I believe I am the first among Western thinkers who has ventured to recognize this crushing result of knowledge....
— From the Preface to *Civilization and Ethics*

Many passages echo the same idea. It was a brave and truthful thing for any man at that time, particularly a pastor, to dispense with Divine Patterns without, at some time, succumbing to disillusionment and cynicism.

Since that time our understanding of the physical universe has been changing. What we know now about the formation of matter, the origin of the stellar system, the operation of the brain, and so on are far from complete, but they are totally different from what Schweitzer knew at the time of the First World War. Any belief about man based on man's relationship with

*the physical universe has been irreparably shattered time and
again in the intervening years, as Darwin and others shattered
the beliefs of the nineteenth century. All we have is ourselves, in
whom we may or may not find something we call divine. Where
other prophets and philosophers have repeatedly become out of
fashion, Schweitzer's elemental discoveries are still valid. The
man whom many regard as old-fashioned is still up-to-date.*

•

*One of the difficulties about Reverence for Life is that it seems
so extraordinarily naïve. Schweitzer believed in and trusted
naïveté, but at first sight this is so over-simple as to be meaningless. Not until one begins to consider the consequences of
living by such a simple belief does one realize its potency.*

*Attempts were made from time to time to persuade Schweitzer
to tabulate Reverence for Life, laying down an order of priority
among creatures. But he refused. To ask for a scale of values in
fact implies a considerable misunderstanding of the whole idea
of Reverence for Life. Reverence is an attitude of mind, not a set
of rules. Schweitzer was asking that people should follow him
in sinking into their own minds and hearts and finding there, as
he was convinced they would, a place where separateness from
other life ceased and solidarity began. Once there, they would not
need rules. Each person would have to make decisions from time
to time about the relative importance to him or her of different
creatures. To keep alive a fallen nestling you must find worms.
To keep a falcon you must sacrifice mice. Each decision must be
personal, but must be made under the overall guidance of Reverence for Life. Nothing must be arbitrary or irresponsible. The
moment you publish a list of priorities you take away that personal responsibility, that fresh openness of heart and spontaneity
of reaction that is of the essence of Schweitzer's thinking.*

*Responsibility is a hard thing. Most people prefer to accept
some common code of behavior that takes from them the need
to make choices. Schweitzer was the ultimate revolutionary who*

would not take orders even from revolutionaries but only from his own conscience, and asks only that others do the same.

It is not by receiving instruction about agreement between ethical and necessary, that a man makes progress in ethics, but only by coming to hear more and more plainly the voice of the ethical, by becoming ruled more and more by the longing to preserve and promote life, and by becoming more and more obstinate in resistance to the necessity for destroying or injuring life.

In ethical conflicts man can arrive only at subjective decisions. No one can decide for him at what point, on each occasion, lies the extreme limit of possibility for his persistence in the preservation and furtherance of life. He alone has to judge this issue, by letting himself be guided by a feeling of the highest possible responsibility towards other life....

We must never let ourselves become blunted. We are living in truth, when we experience these conflicts more profoundly. The good conscience is an invention of the devil.

— *Civilization and Ethics*

But oneself is also part of life, demanding reverence. As the second great commandment of Jesus was to love your neighbor as yourself, implying that you must love yourself before you can love your neighbor, so Reverence for Life can operate from a secure foundation only if the life of others is valued as a result of valuing one's own. In Civilization and Ethics *Schweitzer makes this point clearly and with power:*

Why do I forgive anyone? Ordinary ethics say, because I feel sympathy with him. They allow men, when they pardon others, to seem to themselves wonderfully good, and allow them to practice a style of pardoning which is not free from humiliation of the other. They thus make forgiveness a sweetened triumph of self-devotion.

The ethics of reverence for life do away with this crude point of view. All acts of forbearance and of pardon are for them acts forced from one by sincerity towards oneself. I must practice unlimited forgiveness because, if I did not, I should be wanting in sincerity to myself, for I would be acting as if I myself were not guilty in the same way as the other has been guilty towards me. Because my life is so liberally spotted with falsehood, I must forgive falsehood which has been practiced upon me; because I myself have been in so many cases wanting in love, and guilty of hatred, slander, deceit, or arrogance, I must pardon any want of love and all hatred, slander, deceit, or arrogance which have been directed against myself. I must forgive quietly and unostentatiously; in fact I do not really pardon at all, for I do not let things develop to any such act of judgment. Nor is this any eccentric proceeding; it is only a necessary widening and refining of ordinary ethics.... It is not from kindness to others that I am gentle, peaceable, forbearing, and friendly, but because by such behavior I prove my own profoundest self-realization to be true. Reverence for life which I apply to my own existence, and reverence for life which keeps me in a temper of devotion to other existence than my own, interpenetrate each other.

— *Civilization and Ethics*

In this philosophy there is nothing negative, nothing repressive or divisive, there is no conflict either between man and beast, man and man, or man and himself.

The liberating effect of Reverence for Life makes it the enemy of every form of establishment, every authoritarian code of ethics — including the Marxism that was becoming prevalent while Schweitzer was writing. He wrote in his autobiography:

With the spirit of the age I am in complete disagreement because it is filled with disdain for thinking.... The organized political, social, and religious associations of our time are at work to induce the individual man not to arrive at his convictions by his own thinking, but to make his own the convictions that they keep ready-made for him. Any man who thinks for himself and at the same time is spiritually free is to them something inconvenient and even uncanny.   — *My Life and Thought*

It is impossible to succeed in developing the ethic of ethical personality into a serviceable ethics of society. It seems so obvious, that from right individual ethics right social ethics should result, the one system continuing itself into the other like a town into suburbs. In reality however, they cannot be so built that the streets of the one continue into those of the other. The plans of each are drawn on principles which take no account of that.

The ethic of ethical personality is personal, incapable of regulation, and absolute; the system established by society for its prosperous existence is supra-personal, regulated, and relative. Hence the ethical personality cannot surrender to it, but lives always in continuous conflict with it, obliged again and again to oppose it because it finds its focus too short.

In the last analysis, the antagonism between the two arises from their differing valuations of humaneness. Humaneness consists in never sacrificing a human being to a purpose. The ethic of ethical personality aims at preserving humaneness. The system established by society is impotent in that respect.

When the individual is faced with the alternative of having to sacrifice in some way or other the happiness or the existence of another, or else to bear the loss himself, he is in a position to obey the demands of ethics and to choose the latter. But society, thinking impersonally and pursuing its aims impersonally, does not allow the same weight to consideration for the happiness or existence of an individual. In principle humaneness is not an item in its ethics. But individuals come continually into the position of being in one way or another executive organs of society, and then the conflict between the two points of view becomes active. That this may always be decided in its own favor, society exerts itself as much as possible to limit the authority of the ethic of personality, although inwardly it has to acknowledge its superiority. It wants to have servants who will never oppose it.

Even a society whose ethical standard is relatively high is dangerous to the ethics of its members. If those things which form precisely the defects of a social code of ethics develop strongly, and if society exercises, further, an excessively strong spiritual influence on individuals, then the ethic of ethical personality is ruined. This happens in present-day society, whose ethical conscience is becoming fatally stunted by a biologico-sociological ethic, and this, moreover, finally corrupted by nationalism.

The great mistake of ethical thought down to the present time is that it fails to admit the essential difference between the morality of ethical personality and that which is established from the standpoint of society, and always thinks that it ought, and is able, to cast them in one piece. The result is that the ethic of personality is sacrificed to the ethic of society. And an end must be put to this. What matters is to recognize that the two are engaged in a conflict which cannot be made less intense. Either the moral standard of personality raises the moral standard of society, so far as is possible, to its own level, or it is dragged down by it.   — *Civilization and Ethics*

Happily, the young of today, or at least a large and articulate body of them all over the world, have like Schweitzer come out wholeheartedly for individual responsibility and for life as a whole. They have seen, as he did, the lunacy of pretending that we can survive separately. Just as Schweitzer did, they have therefore rejected the traditional ethics that were limited to loyalties to one small community or another, one self-important creed or another. Life itself is precious, and the old divisions that made people kill each other for living in the wrong place or thinking different thoughts are seen as so ridiculous as to be almost incomprehensible.

To determine the extent to which this can be traced directly back to Schweitzer's influence is impossible. What is sure is that the new generation badly needs a prophet who combines mystical insight with common sense and practical knowledge, as Schweitzer does. If they can find a secure foundation from which to go on challenging the nations and institutions that bred them, we have some hope of consolidating the radical change of outlook that alone can master the social and technological turmoil of our age.

Schweitzer's banner, which looked so irrelevant and old-fashioned in the 1920s and 1930s, could well now lead the field. And as he had known for a long time, it can only come from a philosophy based on personal experience, not on theory.

THREE SERMONS

Shortcomings of Theoretical Philosophy

You all know the name of the philosopher Schopenhauer, who tried to convince men in his writings that the greatest wisdom was to see in life nothing but suffering and struggle and distress. I can never open one of his books without asking myself this question: What would have become of him if, instead of retreating with distinction into his ivory tower, far from professional and human contact, he had been forced to take the post of schoolmaster in a poor mountain village, where he would have had the task of turning a haphazard mob of children, with slack habits, into self-respecting men? He would never have written the books that made him famous, never have been surrounded by clouds of incense, nor had the crown of laurels placed on his white locks; but he would have had more understanding; he would have acquired the deep conviction that life is not only a battlefield, but that it is at one and the same time a struggle and a victory.

... These undying words [of Jesus], "Rejoice, for your names are enrolled in heaven," are not spoken to the fortunate nor to those who rest from their labors, but to the combatants, to those whom Jesus Christ has chosen to announce the victory.

— Sermon preached on May 11, 1902

Reverence for Life

And one of the scribes came, and having heard them reasoning together, and perceiving that he had answered them well, asked him, Which is the first commandment of all? And Jesus answered him, The first of all the commandments is, Hear, O Israel; The Lord our God is one Lord: And thou shalt love the Lord thy God with all thy heart, and with all thy soul, and with all thy mind, and with all thy strength: this is the first commandment. And the second is like, namely this, Thou shalt love thy neighbor as thyself. There is none other commandment greater than these. And the scribe said unto him, Well, Master, thou hast said the truth: for there is one God; and there is none other but he: And to love him with all thy heart, and with all thy understanding, and with all thy will, and with all thy strength, and to love thy neighbor as thyself, is more than all whole burnt offerings and sacrifices. And when Jesus saw that he answered discreetly, he said unto him, Thou art not far from the kingdom of God. And no man after that durst ask him any question. (Mark 12:28–34)

The scribe who asks Jesus which commandment is the greatest is in search of knowledge. He wants information about a matter that concerns him, as it does many of his compatriots. In St. Matthew's Gospel, Chapter 22, the scribes pose this question to Jesus in order to tempt him. But the evangelist Mark surely has a better memory when he describes the sympathetic

scene in which Jesus and the scribe for one moment have mutual understanding and look into one another's hearts, and then
go their separate ways.

In those days Israelite thinkers used to discuss the possibility
of tracing all the commandments, both great and small, back to
a single basic law. We, too, have a similar need. What is intrinsic
good? I have read to you the eternal sayings of our Lord about
forgiveness, mercy, love, and all the other characteristics that we
as his disciples should act upon in the world. But we all seem to
feel that these are only separate colors broken down from the
white light of a basic ethical attitude which he requires from us.

Let me ponder this question with you now: What exactly is
this basic ethical attitude? Later I will devote several meditations to questions on Christian ethics about which I have been
thinking in far-off lands, in the loneliness of the jungle, always
with these services here at St. Nicolai's in mind and in the confident hope that someday I might be permitted to speak to you
about them.

The question of the basic ethical attitude is uppermost in our
minds nowadays. We are forced to a recognition that previous
generations and even we ourselves until recently refused to accept. Now we cannot escape it if we would be truthful: the
Christian ethic has never become a power in the world. It has
not sunk deep into the minds of men. It has been accepted only
superficially, acknowledged in theory more than put into practice. Mankind behaves as if the teaching of Jesus did not exist,
as if Christian behavior had no ethical principles at all.

Therefore, constantly repeating the ethical teaching of Jesus
is of no use, nor is expounding it as though it were bound to
win universal acceptance in the end. It is like trying to paint a
wet wall with pretty colors. We first have to create a foundation for the understanding of the teaching and guide our world
to a frame of mind in which the teachings of Jesus have meaning. It is by no means easy to interpret Jesus' teachings so as to
make them practical to daily life. Let us take as an example the

sayings about the greatest of the commandments. What does it mean to love God with all our heart and to do good only out of love for him? Follow up this train of thought and a whole world of new ideas will open. When in life have you chosen to do good out of love for God when you might otherwise have chosen to do evil?

Or take the other commandment: "Love thy neighbor as thyself." Truly, it is wonderful. I could give you the most alluring illustrations to prove it. But can it be done? Suppose you make a resolution to obey it literally, starting tomorrow. What would be the result in a few days?

This is the greatest riddle in Christian ethics. We cannot apply Jesus' teachings directly to our lives, however holy our desire to serve him. Our frustration then leads us to the great danger of making a reverent bow toward Jesus' words, praising them as the "ideal," but in reality leaving them unheeded.

Still another misunderstanding endangers the realization of Christian morality. A certain ethical attitude can easily make us arrogant. If we forgive our enemies, we think we are being virtuous. If we help a man who needs our assistance, we consider ourselves very noble indeed. We perform small acts of goodness possibly in the name of Christ, considering our deeds somehow different and better than those of other men. Thus we acquire a superior and complacent attitude which actually makes us more unethical than those who do not acknowledge the commandments of Jesus or try to live up to them. The demands of Jesus are difficult just because they require us to do something extraordinary. At the same time he asks us to regard these as something usual, ordinary. While the unusual is exactly what he demands of us. For he says that we should regard ourselves as unprofitable servants, however much we may have accomplished.

So there you have it. Now you know why we must think together about the intrinsic good. We want to learn to understand how the exalted demands of Jesus can be carried out in daily life. We wish to take them as the natural duty of man although they are so exalted in fact.

We want to grasp the underlying principle of all ethics and use that principle as the supreme law from which all ethical actions can be derived. Yes, but can morality be grasped at all? Is it not a matter of the heart? Does it not rest upon love? This we have been told again and again for two thousand years. And what is the result?

Let us study men around us both collectively and individually. Why are they so often unstable? Why are even the most devout among them, and often the pious in particular, capable of being swept by prejudice and passions of nationalism into judgments and courses of action entirely void of ethical truth? Because they lack an ethic based on reason and rooted in logic. Because they do not regard ethics as a natural endowment or as part of their faculty of reason.

Reason and heart must act together if a true morality is to be established. Herein lies the real problem for abstract ethics as well as for practical decisions of daily life. The reason of which I speak penetrates the heart of the matter and embraces the whole of reality, including the realm of the will.

We experience a strange duality when we seek self-understanding in the light of the ethical will within us. On the one hand, we notice its connection with reason. On the other hand, we are forced into decisions that are not rational in ordinary terms but are expressions of demands that would normally be considered extravagant. In this duality, in this strange tension, lies the essence of ethics. We need not fear that an ethic based on reason is geared too low, that it may be too detached and heartless. For when reason really reaches the core of the matter it ceases to be cold reason, whether it wants to or not, and begins to speak with the melody of the heart. And the heart, when it tries to fathom itself, discovers that its realm overlaps the realm of reason. It has to pass through the land of reason to reach the furthest boundary of its own superfluous sphere. How can that be?

Let us explore the basic principle of goodness both from the heart's point of view and then from reason's point of view, and see where both meet.

The heart maintains that ethics is based on love. Let us explore this word. "Love" means harmony of being, community of being. Originally it applied to groups or persons who in some way belonged to one another, who had an inner reciprocal relationship, such as children and parents, married couples, or intimate friends. Morality requires that people we don't know should not be considered as strangers. That applies equally to those who are worse than strangers to us, because we feel an aversion toward them or because they have shown hostility to us. Even such people we must treat as our friends. In the last analysis the commandment of love means this: no one is a stranger to you; every man's welfare is your concern. We so often take for granted that some people are our immediate concern while others are a matter of indifference to us. Clearly this natural feeling is not permitted by ethical standards. Jesus rules out behaving toward one another as strangers when he says, "The other man must mean as much to you as your own self. You must feel his welfare as your own direct concern."

Further, let the heart explain the first commandment: "Thou shalt love thy God with all thy heart and with all thy mind and with all thy strength." To love God — this remote, unfathomable being! Here it is plain that the word "love," used ethically, is meant in a figurative sense. Should God, who has no need of us, be loved as though he were a creature we meet in daily life? In a human context, love means, for example, sharing an experience, showing compassion, and helping one another. But our love of God is akin to reverent love. God is infinite life. Thus the most elementary ethical principle, when understood by the heart, means that out of reverence for the unfathomable, infinite, and living Reality we call God, we must never consider ourselves strangers toward any human being. Rather, we must bind ourselves to the task of sharing his experiences and try being of help to him.

That, then, is what the heart says when it tries to give meaning to the command of love toward God and neighbor.

But now let reason speak. Let us pretend that we have learned nothing about ethics from the past and see how far we can get by pondering the forces that influence our actions. Can reason, too, make us step outside ourselves? People often say that only egotism can be justified by reason. What can I do to have it easy? That is their reason's wisdom, nothing else. At most it can teach us a certain integrity and justice, and these things are more or less the recognized key to happiness. Reason is the desire for knowledge and the desire for happiness, and both are mysteriously connected with one another, in an inward way.

Desire for wisdom! Explore everything around you, penetrate to the furthest limits of human knowledge, and always you will come up against something inexplicable in the end. It is called life. It is a mystery so inexplicable that the knowledge of the educated and the ignorant is purely relative when contemplating it.

What is the difference between the scientist who observes in his microscope the most minute and unexpected signs of life, and the old farmer who by contrast can barely read or write, who stands in springtime in his garden and contemplates the buds opening on the branches of his trees? Both are confronted with the riddle of life. One may be able to describe life in greater detail, but for both it remains equally inscrutable. All knowledge is, in the final analysis, the knowledge of life. All realization is amazement at this riddle of life — a reverence for life in its infinite and yet ever-fresh manifestations. How amazing this coming into being, living, and dying! How fantastic that in other existences something comes into being, passes away again, comes into being once more, and so forth from eternity to eternity! How can it be? We can do all things, and we can do nothing. For in all our wisdom we cannot create life. What we create is dead.

Life means strength, will, arising from the abyss, dissolving into the abyss again. Life is feeling, experience, suffering. If you study life deeply, looking with perceptive eyes into the vast animated chaos of this creation, its profundity will seize you suddenly with dizziness. In everything you recognize yourself. The tiny beetle that lies dead in your path — it was a living creature, struggling for existence like yourself, rejoicing in the sun like you, knowing fear and pain like you. And now it is no more than decaying matter — which is what you will be sooner or later, too.

You walk outside and it is snowing. You carelessly shake the snow from your sleeves. It attracts your attention: a lacy snowflake glistens in your hand. You can't help looking at it. See how it sparkles in a wonderfully intricate pattern. Then it quivers, and the delicate needles of which it consists contract. It melts and lies dead in your hand. It is no more. The snowflake which fluttered down from infinite space upon your hand, where it sparkled and quivered and died — that is yourself. Wherever you see life — that is yourself!

What is this recognition, this knowledge within the reach of the most scientific and the most childlike? It is reverence for life, reverence for the unfathomable mystery we confront in our universe, an existence different in its outward appearance and yet inwardly of the same character as our own, terribly similar, awesomely related. The strangeness between us and other creatures is here removed. Reverence for the infinity of life means removal of the alienation, restoration of empathy, compassion, sympathy. And so the final result of knowledge is the same as that required of us by the commandment of love. Heart and reason agree together when we desire and dare to be men who seek to fathom the depths of the universe.

Reason discovers the bridge between love for God and love for men — love for all creatures, reverence for all being, compassion with all life, however dissimilar to our own.

I cannot but have reverence for all that is called life. I cannot avoid compassion for everything that is called life. That is the beginning and foundation of morality. Once a man has experienced it and continues to do so — and he who has once experienced it will continue to do so — he is ethical. He carries his morality within him and can never lose it, for it continues to develop within him. He who has never experienced this has only a set of superficial principles. These theories have no root in him, they do not belong to him, and they fall off him. The worst is that the whole of our generation had only such a set of superficial principles. Then the time came to put the ethical code to the test, and it evaporated. For centuries the human race had been educated with only a set of superficial principles. We were brutal, ignorant, and heartless without being aware of it. We had no scale of values, for we had no reverence for life.

It is our duty to share and maintain life. Reverence concerning all life is the greatest commandment in its most elementary form. Or expressed in negative terms: "Thou shalt not kill." We take this prohibition so lightly, thoughtlessly plucking a flower, thoughtlessly stepping on a poor insect, thoughtlessly, in terrible blindness because everything takes its revenge, disregarding the suffering and lives of our fellow men, sacrificing them to trivial earthly goals.

Much talk is heard in our times about building a new human race. How are we to build a new humanity? Only by leading men toward a true, inalienable ethic of our own, which is capable of further development. But this goal cannot be reached unless countless individuals will transform themselves from blind men into seeing ones and begin to spell out the great commandment which is: Reverence for Life. Existence depends more on reverence for life than the law and the prophets. Reverence for life comprises the whole ethic of love in its deepest and highest sense. It is the source of constant renewal for the individual and for mankind.

—Sermon preached at St. Nicolai's Church,
February 16, 1919

Ethics of Compassion

For none of us liveth to himself, and no man dieth to himself.   (Romans 14:7)

As I suggested last Sunday, we shall be discussing the problems of ethics in our next service.

When the scribe asked what was the greatest commandment in the Old Testament, Jesus replied by combining two precepts — love of God and love of neighbor. This, as we saw last week, raises the question of the nature of ethics, of the ultimate, fundamental principle of morality. We were not satisfied with the age-old answer that the essence of ethics is love. We went on to ask what love really is. What is the sort of love toward God which compels us to be kind to others? What does love for our neighbor mean? And we asked not only the heart but also the reason to explain the ethical. For, as we saw, the weakness of our times lies in a lack of a morality based on reason, a failure to discover an ethic immune to prejudice and passion. We never assume that reason and heart can walk effortlessly hand in hand. But the true heart is rational and the true reason has sensitivity. As we noticed, both heart and reason agree that in the last resort the good consists in elemental reverence of the enigma we call life, in reverence for all its manifestations, both great and small. The good is what preserves and advances life; evil is what hinders or destroys it. We are ethical if we abandon our stubbornness, if we surrender our strangeness toward other creatures and share in the life and the suffering that surround us. Only this quality makes us truly human. Only then do we possess an inalienable, continuously developing, and self-orienting ethic of our own.

"Reverence for life," "surrender of strangeness," "the urge to maintain life" — we hear these expressions around us, and they sound cold and shallow. But even if they are modest words they are rich in meaning. A seed is equally commonplace and insignificant, yet within it rests the germ of a lovely flower or a life-giving food. These simple words contain the basic attitude from which all ethical behavior develops, whether the individual is conscious of it or not. Thus the presupposition of morality is to share everything that goes on around us, not only in human life but in the life of all creatures. This awareness forces us to do all within our power for the preservation and advancement of life.

The great enemy of morality has always been indifference. As children, as far as our awareness of things went, we had an elementary capacity for compassion. But our capacity did not develop over the years in proportion to the growth of our understanding. This was uncomfortable and bewildering. We noticed so many people who no longer had compassion or empathy. Then we, too, suppressed our sensitivity so as to be like everyone else. We did not want to be different from them, and we did not know what to do. Thus many people become like houses in which one story after another has been vacated, a lifeless structure in which all windows look empty and strange, deserted.

To remain good means to remain wide awake. We are all like men walking in the bitter cold and snow. Woe to him who gives way to exhaustion, sits down, and falls asleep. He will never wake again. So our inmost moral being perishes when we are too tired to share the life and experiences and sufferings of the creatures around us. Woe to us if our sensitivity grows numb. It destroys our conscience in the broadest sense of the word: the consciousness of how we should act dies.

Reverence for life and sympathy with other lives is of supreme importance for this world of ours. Nature knows no similar reverence for life. It produces life a thousand-fold in the most meaningful way and destroys it a thousand-fold in the most meaningless way. In every stage of life, right up to the level of man, terrible ignorance lies over all creatures. They have the will to live but no capacity for compassion toward other creatures. They can't feel what happens inside others. They suffer but have no compassion. The great struggle for survival by which nature is maintained is in strange contradiction with itself. Creatures live at the expense of other creatures. Nature permits the most horrible cruelties to be committed. It impels insects by their instincts to bore holes into other insects, to lay their eggs in them so that maggots may grow there and live off the caterpillar, thus causing it a slow and painful death. Nature lets ants band together to attack poor little creatures and hound them to death. Look at the spider. How gruesome is the craft that nature taught it!

Nature looks beautiful and marvelous when you view it from the outside. But when you read its pages like a book, it is horrible. And its cruelty is so senseless! The most precious form of life is sacrificed to the lowliest. A child breathes the germs of tuberculosis. He grows and flourishes but is destined to suffering and a premature death because these lowly creatures multiply in his vital organs. How often in Africa have I been overcome with horror when I examined the blood of a patient who was suffering from sleeping sickness. Why did this man, his face contorted in pain, have to sit in front of me, groaning, "Oh, my head, my head"? Why should he have to suffer night after night and die a wretched death? Because there, under the microscope, were minute, pale corpuscles, one ten-thousandth of a millimeter long — not very many, sometimes such a very few that one had to look for hours to find them at all.

This, then, is the enigmatic contradiction in the will to live — life against life, causing suffering and death, innocent and yet guilty. Nature teaches cruel egotism, only briefly interrupted

by the urge it has planted in creatures to offer love and assistance for their offspring as long as necessary. Animals love
their young so much that they are willing to die for them. They
have this capacity for sympathy. Yet the self-perpetuation of the
species makes all the more terrible their utter lack of concern
for those beings unrelated to them.

The world given over to ignorance and egotism is like a valley shrouded in darkness. Only up on the peaks is there light.
All must live in the darkness. Only one creature can escape and
catch a glimpse of the light: the highest creature, man. He is permitted to achieve the knowledge of reverence for life. His is the
privilege of achieving the knowledge of shared experience and
compassion, of transcending the ignorance in which the rest of
creation pines. And this understanding is the great event in the
evolution of life. Through it truth and goodness appear in the
world. Light shines above the darkness. The highest form of life
has been attained, life sharing the life of others, in which one
existence feels the pulse of the whole world and life becomes
aware of its all-embracing existence. Individual isolation ceases.
Outside life streams like a flood into our own.

We live in the world, and the world lives in us. Even this
knowledge raises a host of questions. Why do the laws of nature
and the laws of ethics diverge so sharply? Why cannot human
reason simply take over and develop its discoveries into an expression of life in nature? Why must rationality come into such
terrible conflict with everything it sees? Why must it discover
that the law of its own being is so utterly different from the
laws governing the world? Why must it be at odds with the
world just when it discovers the principle of the good? Why
must we experience this conflict without the hope of ever finding solution? Why, instead of harmony, is there cleavage? And
further, God is the power that sustains the universe. Why is this
God who reveals himself in nature the denial of everything we
feel to be ethical? How can a force rationally create life and ir-
rationally destroy it at the same time? How can we reconcile

God as a force of nature with God as ethical will, the God of love as we must conceive him when we have risen to a higher ideal of life, to reverence for life, to empathy and compassion?

Several Sundays ago, when we were trying to clarify optimistic and pessimistic views of life, I told you that it is a great misfortune for mankind that we cannot offer a harmonious philosophy of life. The more knowledge increases, the more it deprives us of such a possibility. Not only because it becomes increasingly plain how little we can grasp in knowledge, but also because the contradictions in life become increasingly evident. We know in part, as St. Paul says. But this is not putting it strongly enough. The greater obstacle is that our knowledge affords only a glimpse into insoluble contradictions, all of which can be traced back to the one basic contradiction: the law according to which all this illogic occurs has, in itself, nothing that we recognize and feel to be ethical.

Instead of being able to anchor our morality in a coherent worldview and a harmonious concept of God, we must constantly defend it against the contradictions arising from our worldview, contradictions that threaten it like a destructive breaker. We must erect a dam — but will it hold?

The other threat to our capacity and our will to empathy is nagging doubt. What is the use of it?, you think. Your most strenuous efforts to prevent suffering, to ease suffering, to preserve life, are nothing compared to the anguish remaining in the world around you, the wounds you are powerless to heal. Certainly, it is dreadful to be reminded of the extent of our helplessness. It is worse still to realize how much suffering we ourselves cause others without being able to prevent it.

You are walking along a path in the woods. The sunshine makes lovely patterns through the trees. The birds are singing, and thousands of insects buzz happily in the air. But as you walk along the path, you are involuntarily the cause of death. Here you trod on an ant and tortured it; there you squashed a beetle; and over there your unknowing step left a worm

writhing in agony. Into the glorious melody of life you weave a
discordant strain of suffering and death. You are guilty, though
it is no fault of your own. And, despite all your good intentions,
you are conscious of a terrible inability to help as you would
like to. Then comes the voice of the tempter: Why torture yourself? It is no good. Give up, stop caring. Be unconcerned and
unfeeling like everybody else.

Still another temptation arises — compassion really involves
you in suffering. Anyone who experiences the woes of this
world within his heart can never again feel the surface happiness that human nature desires. When hours of contentment
and joy come, the compassionate man cannot give himself un-
reservedly to them, for he can never forget the suffering he has
experienced with others. What he has seen stays with him. The
anguished faces of the poor return; the cries of the sick echo in
his mind; he remembers the man whose hard lot he once read
about — and darkness shuts out the light of his joy. Darkness
returns again and again. In cheerful company he suddenly becomes absentminded. And the tempter says again: You can't
live like this. You must be able to detach yourself from what
is depressing around you. Don't be so sensitive. Teach yourself
the necessary indifference, put on an armor, be thoughtless like
everybody else if you want to live a sensible life. In the end
we are ashamed to know of the great experience of empathy
and compassion. We keep it secret from one another and pretend it is foolish, a weakness we outgrow when we begin to be
"reasonable" people.

These three great temptations unobtrusively wreck the presupposition of all goodness. Guard against them. Counter the
first temptation by saying that for you to share experience and
to lend a helping hand is an absolute inward necessity. Your utmost attempts will be but a drop in the ocean compared with
what needs to be done, but only this attitude will give meaning
and value to your life. Wherever you are, as far as you can, you
should bring redemption, redemption from the misery brought

into the world by the self-contradictory will of life, redemption that only he who has this knowledge can bring. The small amount you are able to do is actually much if it only relieves pain, suffering, and fear from any living being, be it human or any other creature. The preservation of life is the true joy.

As for the other temptation, the fear that compassion will involve you in suffering, counter it with the realization that the sharing of sorrow expands your capacity to share joy as well. When you callously ignore the suffering of others, you lose the capacity to share their happiness, too. And however little joy we may see in this world, the sharing of it, together with the good we ourselves create, produces the only happiness which makes life tolerable. And finally, you have no right to say: I will be this, or I will be that, because I think one way will make me happier than another. No, you must be what you ought to be, a true, knowing man, a man who identifies himself with the world, a man who experiences the world within himself. Whether you are happier by the ordinary standards of happiness or not doesn't matter. The secret hour does not require of us that we should be happy — to obey the call is the only thing that satisfies deeply.

So I tell you, don't let your hearts grow numb. Stay alert. It is your soul which matters. If only these words — words in which I am laying bare my inmost thoughts — could force you who are with me here to destroy the deceit with which the world tries to put us to sleep! If only you would all stop being thoughtless and stop flinching from the challenge to learn reverence for life and true empathy, if only you could be absorbed in compassionate awareness, I would rest content. I would consider my work blessed, even if I knew I would not be allowed to preach tomorrow or that my preaching thus far had been useless or that I would never again be able to achieve anything else.

I who generally shrink from influencing others, because of the responsibility it entails, now wish I had the power to transform you, and make you have compassion, until each one of

you had experienced the great suffering from which there is
no escape and had gained the wisdom that compassion brings.
Then I could tell myself that you are on the way to real goodness and that you will never lose it again. None of us lives for
himself. May this word pursue us. May it never let us rest until
we are laid into our graves.

— Sermon preached at St. Nicolai's Church,
February 23, 1919

THE ETHICS OF REVERENCE FOR LIFE

*In 1936 Albert Schweitzer published this article in the periodi-
cal* Christendom *(1 [1936]: 225–39), as a general discussion of
the ethics of reverence for life. The article rehearses many familiar aspects of Schweitzer's ethic. Particularly noteworthy are
Schweitzer's suggestions about how ethics is rooted in physical
life and his anecdotes about ethical geese, monkeys, and sparrows. Also reprinted in Henry Clark,* The Ethical Mysticism of
Albert Schweitzer *(Boston: Beacon Press, 1962), 180–94, the
article is reproduced here (modified slightly for style) with the
permission of the World Council of Churches.*

In the history of world thought we seem to be met by a confusion of antagonistic systems. But if we look closely, we see that
certain essential laws of thought are to be discerned. And as we
trace them, we see a certain definite progress in this bewildering
history. In fact, there emerge two main classes of problems. To
begin with, we see certain facade problems, important looking,
but not really connected with the main structure. Questions as
to the reality of the world and the problem of knowledge belong here. Kant tried in vain to solve the essential questions by
busying himself with these scientific, facade problems. Admittedly they are intriguing, but they are not the real, elementary
matters.

We are concerned with the other problems, the essential ones. As we know life in ourselves, we want to understand life in the universe, in order to enter into harmony with it. Physically we are always trying to do this. But that is not the primary matter; for the great issue is that we shall achieve a spiritual harmony. Just to recognize this fact is to have begun to see a part of life clearly.

There is in each of us the will-to-live, which is based on the mystery of what we call "taking an interest." We cannot live alone. Though someone is an egoist, he or she is never completely so. He must always have some interest in life about him. If for no other reason, he must do so in order to make his own life more perfect. Thus it happens that we want to devote ourselves; we want to take our part in perfecting our ideal of progress; we want to give meaning to the life in the world. This is the basis of our striving for harmony with the spiritual element.

The effort for harmony, however, never succeeds. Events cannot be harmonized with our activities. Working purposefully toward certain ends, we assume that the Creative Force in the world is doing likewise. Yet, when we try to define its goal, we cannot do so. It tends toward developing a type of existence, but there is no coordinated, definite end to be observed, even though we think there should be. We like to imagine that humankind is nature's goal; but facts do not support that belief.

Indeed, when we consider the immensity of the universe, we must confess that humankind is insignificant. The world began, as it were, yesterday. It may end tomorrow. Life has existed in the universe but a brief second. And certainly human life can hardly be considered the goal of the universe. Its margin of existence is always precarious. Study of the geologic periods shows that. So does the battle against disease. When one has seen whole populations annihilated by sleeping sickness, as I have, one ceases to imagine that human life is nature's goal. In fact, the Creative Force does not concern itself about preserving life. It simultaneously creates and destroys. Therefore, the will-to-live is not to be understood within the circle of Creative Force. Philosophy and religion have repeatedly sought the solution by this road; they have projected our will to perfection into nature at large, expecting to see its counterpart there. But in all honesty we must confess that to cling to such a belief is to delude ourselves.

As a result of the failure to find ethics reflected in the natural order, the disillusioned cry has been raised that ethics can therefore have no ultimate validity. In the world of human thought and action today, humanitarianism is definitely on the wane. Brutality and trust in force are in the ascendant. What, then, is to become of that vigorous ethics which we inherited from our parents?

Knowledge may have failed us, but we do not abandon the ideals. Though they are shaken, we do not turn from them to sheer skepticism. In spite of being unable to prove them by rational argumentation, we nevertheless believe that there is a proof and defense for them within themselves. We are, so to speak, immunized against skepticism. Indeed, the classical skepticisms were, after all, puerile. That a truth cannot be proved by argument is no reason why it should be utterly abandoned, so long as it is in itself possessed of value. Kant, trying to escape from skepticism, is a pre-indication of this immunity. In intent, his philosophy is great and eternal. He said that truth is one of two kinds: scientific and spiritual. Let us look to the bottom of this, not by Kant's method, however, since he was often content with naïve reflections on very deep questions. We shall avoid his way of seeking abstract solutions and distinctions between material and immaterial. Instead, let us see that truths which are not provable in knowledge are given to us in our will-to-live.

Kant sought to give equal value to practical and theoretical reason. More, he felt the demand for a more absolute ethic.

It would, he thought, give new authority to spiritual and religious truth, thus making up for the loss involved in not being able to verify these truths by knowledge. This is the very heart of Kant's gospel, being much more important than anything he taught about space and time. But he did not know where to find the new ethic. He only gave a new, more handsome, and more impressive facade to the old. By his failure to point out the new ethic, he missed the new rationalism. His thought was on too narrow a basis.

1. The essential thing to realize about ethics is that it is the very manifestation of our will-to-live. All our thoughts are given in that will-to-live, and we but give them expression and form in words. To analyze reason fully would be to analyze the will-to-live. The philosophy that abandons the old rationalism must begin by meditating on itself. Thus, if we ask, "What is the immediate fact of my consciousness? What do I self-consciously know of myself, making abstractions of all else, from childhood to old age? To what do I always return?" we find the simple fact of consciousness is this, I will to live. Through every stage of life, this is the one thing I know about myself. I do not say, "I am life," for life continues to be a mystery too great to understand. I only know that I cling to it. I fear its cessation — death. I dread its diminution — pain. I seek its enlargement — joy.

Descartes started on this basis. But he built an artificial structure by presuming a person knows nothing and doubts all, whether outside himself or within. And in order to end doubt, he fell back on the fact of consciousness: I think. Surely, however, that is the stupidest primary assumption in all philosophy! Who can establish the fact that he thinks, except in relation to thinking something? And what that something is, is the important matter. When I seek the first fact of consciousness, it is not to know that I think, but to get hold of myself. Descartes would have a person think once, just long enough to establish certainty of being, and then give over any further need of meditation. Yet meditation is the very thing I must not cease. I must ascertain whether my thoughts are in harmony with my will-to-live.

Bergson's admirable philosophy also starts from such a beginning. But he arrives at the sense of time. The fact of immediate consciousness, however, is much more important than the sense of time. So Bergson misses the real issue.

Instinct, thought, the capacity for divination, all these are fused in the will-to-live. And when it reflects upon itself, what path does it follow? When my will-to-live begins to think, it sees life as a mystery in which I remain by thought. I cling to life because of my reverence for life. For, when it begins to think, the will-to-live realizes that it is free. It is free to leave life. It is free to choose whether or not to live. This fact is of particular significance for us in this modern age, when there are abundant possibilities for abandoning life, painlessly and without agony.

Moreover, we are all closer to the possibility of this choice than we may guess of one another. The question which haunts men and women today is whether life is worth living. Perhaps each of us has had the experience of talking with a friend one day, finding that person bright, happy, apparently in the full joy of life; and then the next day we find that he has taken his own life! Stoicism has brought us to this point, by driving out the fear of death; for by inference it suggests that we are free to choose whether to live or not. But if we entertain such a possibility, we do so by ignoring the melody of the will-to-live, which compels us to face the mystery, the value, the high trust committed to us in life. We may not understand it, but we begin to appreciate its great value. Therefore, when we find those who relinquish life, while we may not condemn them, we do pity them for having ceased to be in possession of themselves. Ultimately, the issue is not whether we do or do not fear death. The real issue is that of reverence for life.

Here, then, is the first spiritual act in someone's experience: reverence for life. The consequence of it is that one comes to realize his dependence upon events quite beyond his control.

Therefore he becomes resigned. And this is the second spiritual act: resignation.

What happens is that one realizes that he is but a speck of dust, a plaything of events outside his reach. Nevertheless, he may at the same time discover that he has a certain liberty, as long as he lives. Sometime or another all of us must have found that happy events have not been able to make us happy, nor unhappy events to make us unhappy. There is within each of us a modulation, an inner exaltation, which lifts us above the buffetings with which events assail us. Likewise, it lifts us above dependence upon the gifts of events for our joy. Hence, our dependence upon events is not absolute; it is qualified by our spiritual freedom. Therefore, when we speak of resignation it is not sadness to which we refer, but the triumph of our will-to-live over whatever happens to us. And to become ourselves, to be spiritually alive, we must have passed beyond this point of resignation.

The great defect of modern philosophy is that it neglects this essential fact. It does not ask someone to think deeply on himself. It hounds him into activity, bidding him find escape thus. In that respect it falls far below the philosophy of Greece, which taught people better the true depth of life.

I have said that resignation is the very basis of ethics. Starting from this position, the will-to-live comes first to veracity as the primary ground of virtue. If I am faithful to my will-to-live, I cannot disguise this fact, even though such disguise or evasion might seem to my advantage. Reverence for my will-to-live leads me to the necessity of being sincere with myself. And out of this fidelity to my own nature grows all my faithfulness. Thus, sincerity is the first ethical quality which appears. However lacking one may be in other respects, sincerity is the one thing which he must possess. Nor is this point of view to be found only among people of complex social life. Primitive cultures show the fact to be equally true there. Resignation to the will-to-live leads directly to this first virtue: sincerity.

2. Having reached this point, then, I am in a position to look at the world. I ask knowledge what it can tell me of life. Knowledge replies that what it can tell me is little, yet immense. Whence this universe came, or whither it is bound, or how it happens to be at all, knowledge cannot tell me. Only this: that the will-to-live is everywhere present, even as in me. I do not need science to tell me this; but it cannot tell me anything more essential. Profound and marvelous as chemistry is, for example, it is like all science in the fact that it can lead me only to the mystery of life, which is essentially in me, however near or far away it may be observed.

What shall be my attitude toward this other life? It can only be of a piece with my attitude toward my own life. If I am a thinking being, I must regard other life than my own with equal reverence. For I shall know that it longs for fullness and development as deeply as I do myself. Therefore, I see that evil is what annihilates, hampers, or hinders life. And this holds good whether I regard it physically or spiritually. Goodness, by the same token, is the saving or helping of life, the enabling of whatever life I can to attain its highest development.

This is the absolute and reasonable ethic. Whether such-and-such a person arrives at this principle, I may not know. But I know that it is given inherently in the will-to-live. Whatever is reasonable is good. This we have been told by all the great thinkers. But it reaches its best only in the light of this universal ethic, the ethic of reverence for life, to which we come as we meditate upon the will-to-live. And since it is important that we recognize to the best of our ability the full significance of this ethic, let us now devote our attention to some commentaries upon it.

Our first commentary: the primary characteristic of this ethic is that it is rational, having been developed as a result of thought upon life.

We may say that anyone who truly explores the depths of thought must arrive at this point. In other words, to be truly rational is to become ethical. (How pleased Socrates would be with us for saying this!) But if it is so simple a matter of rationality, why has it not long since been achieved? It has, indeed, been long on the way, while in every land thought has been seeking to deepen ethics. Actually, whenever love and devotion are glimpsed, reverence for life is not far off, since one grows from the other. But the truth of the matter is that thought fears such an ethic. What it wants is to impose regulations and order that can be duly systematized. This ethic is not subject to such bounding. Therefore, when modern thought considers such an ethic it fears it, and tries to discredit it by calling it irrational. In this way its development has been long delayed.

Again, it may be asked if this sort of meditation is not definitely that of civilized rather than primitive people. The primitive person, it may be argued, knows no such reverence for life. To this I must agree, having associated with primitive people in my work in Africa. Nevertheless, it remains true that the primitive person who begins to meditate must proceed along this same path. He must start with his own will-to-live, and that is certain to bring him in this direction. If he does not reach a point as far along the way as we do, that is because we can profit by the meditations of our predecessors. There are many great souls who have blazed sections of the trail for us. Proceeding along that way, I have led you to this conclusion: that rational processes, properly pursued, must lead to the true ethic.

Another commentary: What of this ethic? Is it absolute?

Kant defines absolute ethics as that which is not concerned with whether it can be achieved. The distinction is not one of absolute as opposed to relative, but absolute as distinct from practicable in the ethical field. An absolute ethic calls for the creating of perfection in this life. It cannot be completely achieved; but that fact does not really matter. In this sense, reverence for life is an absolute ethic. It does not lay down specific rules for each possible situation. It simply tells us that we are responsible for the lives about us. It does not set either minimum or maximum limits to what we must do.

In point of fact, every ethic has something of the absolute about it, just as soon as it ceases to be mere social law. It demands of one what is actually beyond his strength. Take the question of one's duty to his neighbor. The ethic cannot be fully carried out, without involving the possibility of complete sacrifice of self. Yet, philosophy has never bothered to take due notice of the distinction. It has simply tried to ignore absolute ethics, because such ethics cannot be fitted into tabulated rules and regulations. Indeed, the history of world teachings on the subject may be summarized in the motto "Avoid absolute ethics, and thus keep within the realm of the possible."

We have already noted that Kant did postulate and demand an absolute ethics as the foundation for a spiritual ethics. He knew it must be more profound than what is just and reasonable. But he did not succeed in establishing what it was. All he did was label ordinary ethics "absolute." Consequently, he ended in a muddle of abstraction. As Descartes said, "Think," without telling what to think, so Kant demanded, "Observe absolute ethics," without elucidating what the term involved. The ethics he proposed could not be called absolute in matter of content. His "practical ethics" proved to be simply the good old utilitarian ethics of his own day, adorned with the label "absolute." He failed by not thinking far enough. To justify the name, absolute ethics must be so not only in authority, but in matter of content as well. Another commentary: reverence for life is a universal ethic.

We do not say this because of its absolute nature, but because of the boundlessness of its domain. Ordinary ethics seeks to find limits within the sphere of human life and relationships. But the absolute ethics of the will-to-live must reverence every form of life, seeking so far as possible to refrain from destroying any life, regardless of its particular type. It says of no instance of life, "This has no value." It cannot make any such exceptions, for it is built upon reverence for life as such. It knows that the mystery of life is always too profound for us, and that its value is beyond our capacity to estimate. We happen to believe that human life is more important than any other form of which we know. But we cannot prove any such comparison of value from what we know of the world's development. True, in practice we are forced to choose. At times we have to decide arbitrarily which forms of life, and even which particular individuals, we shall save, and which we shall destroy. But the principle of reverence for life is nonetheless universal.

Ordinary ethics has never known what to do with this problem. Not realizing that the domain of ethics must be boundless, it has tried to ignore any absolute ethic. But when its boundlessness is realized, then its absoluteness is more plain. Indian thought recognizes this, but it limits its effectiveness by making ethics negative. The characteristic attitude of Indian thought is less a positive reverence for life than a negative duty to refrain from destroying. This comes about through a failure to appreciate the essentially illusory nature of an ethic of inaction. Nor has European thought been free from that same illusion. The great works on philosophy and ethics in recent years have all tried to avoid absolute ethics by concentrating on a type which should apply only socially. But when reason travels its proper course, it moves in the direction of a universally applicable ethic.

Another commentary: a universal ethic has great spiritual significance. Ordinary ethics is too narrow and shallow for spiritual development.

Our thought seeks ever to attain harmony with the mysterious Spirit of the Universe. To be complete, such harmony must be both active and passive. That is to say, we seek harmony both in deed and in thought. I want to understand my ethical activity as being at the service of the Universal Spirit.

Spinoza, Hegel, and the Stoics show us that the harmony of peace is a passive harmony, to which true philosophy leads us, and toward which religion tries to lead us. But this does not suffice, since we want to be at one in activity as well. Philosophy fails us here because of too narrow an ethical basis. It may seek to put me in relation to society, and even to humanity at large (although contemporary philosophies are in some instances directed only toward the relationship to a nation or a race). In any case, no philosophy puts me in relationship to the universe on an ethical basis. Instead, the attempt is made to take me there by knowledge, through understanding. Fichte and Hegel present such an intellectual philosophy. But it is an impossible path. Such philosophies are bankrupt. Ethics alone can put me in true relationship with the universe by my serving it, cooperating with it, not by trying to understand it. This is why Kant is so profound when he speaks of practical reason. Only by serving every kind of life do I enter the service of that Creative Will whence all life emanates. I do not understand it; but I do know (and it is sufficient to live by) that by serving life, I serve the Creative Will. It is through community of life, not community of thought, that I abide in harmony with that Will. This is the mystical significance of ethics.

Every philosophy has its mystical aspects, and every profound thought is mystical. But mysticism has always stopped with the passive, on an insufficient basis, in regard to ethics. Indian, Stoic, medieval — all the great mysticisms — have aimed at achieving union through passivity. Yet every true mysticism has instincts of activity, aspiring to an ethical character. This fact explains the development of Indian mysticism from the detachment of Brahminism to modern Hindu mysticism. Medieval mysticism, in the same way, comes in its great exponent, Eckhart, to the point where it longs to comprehend true ethics. Failing to find the universal ethic, it has commonly been content to exist with none. But in the universal ethic of reverence for life, mystical union with the Universal Spirit is actually and fully achieved. Thus it is proved to be indeed the true ethic. For it must be plain that an ethic which only commands is incomplete, while one which lets me live in communion with the Creative Will is a true and complete ethic.

3. In what sense is this a natural ethic, and how does it stand in relation to other explanations of the origin of ethics?

There have been three general classifications of ethical origins. The first is a spiritual interpretation. We find in Plato, Kant, and many others the assertion that ethics comes out of an inherent, insubstantial, given sense of duty, which has its source in our own power of reason. Through it, we are told, we see ourselves bound to the immaterial world. The exponents of this view believed that they had thus given great dignity to ethics. But there are difficulties in the way of accepting this view. It bears little resemblance to our own ethical sense; and we cannot see how it can be carried into our lives in this world in which we live.

The second classification comprises the intellectual theories of ethics. Here we find such philosophies as those of the Stoics and Lao-tse. This group claims to see ethics in the natural world, and concludes thereby that whoever is in harmony with the universe is by that fact ethical. Now, this is a grand theory, and it is based on a profound realization that one who is truly in such harmony must be ethical. But the fact remains that we do not indeed understand the Spirit of the Universe. Therefore, we cannot draw any ethics from such understanding. Consequently, these theories of ethics are pallid and lacking in vigor. What they really amount to is a negative quietism, which has been tinged with ethics.

The third classification consists of three kinds of natural ethics. There is, to start with, the suggestion that ethics exists within our very natures, waiting to be developed. It is argued that we are primarily composed of egoism, but that we nevertheless have an inherent selflessness. Altruism, as we know it, is thus simply exalted egoism. A person is assumed to get his greatest fulfillment in society; wherefore, he must serve it, sacrificing his own wishes temporarily. But such an explanation is childish.

Next comes the sort of natural ethics which is said to exist in human nature, but is incapable of being developed by the individual himself. Society, so the theory runs, has worked out a system of ethics in order to subject the individual to its will. Centuries of such exalting of society have had beneficial results, but it is mere delusion to imagine that that is native to us which has actually been created by society. But observe how childish this is also. I grant that society has its place in ethics, but the fact remains that I have individual as well as social relationships, and society simply cannot be responsible for the ethic which determines my dealings in the individual sphere.

The third type of natural ethics was expounded by Hume. It admits that ethics is a matter of sentiment, but explains that it is given in the nature of a human being, for the sake of preserving his life. Thus, in the late eighteenth century came Hume's teaching that ethics is natural, while in the same period came Kant's realization that it must be absolute.

To explain that ethics is a matter of feeling, prompted by our own hearts, Hume called it sympathy. The capacity to understand and live others' lives in our own is, he said, what makes us developed individuals. In this, he was joined by George Adam Smith. They were headed in the right direction, too. If they had properly explored sympathy, they would have reached the universal ethic of reverence for life. But they stopped on the very threshold of their great opportunity, because they were dominated by the contemporary dogma that ethics is concerned only with the relationship of human being to human being. Therefore, they twisted sympathy to mean only a relationship between like kinds. Spencer and Darwin did the same thing in their time, putting ethics on the basis of the herd. This brought them to the explanation of non-egoistic action as arising from herd instinct. What Darwin failed to see is that the herd relationship is more than this superficial sort of instinct. He did, it is true, catch a glimpse of the possibility of sympathy extending beyond the range of humankind and society. But he concluded that it was just a high development of the herd instinct!

It is only when we break loose from such traditions that we find sympathy to be natural for any type of life, without any restrictions, so long as we are capable of imagining in such life the characteristic which we find in our own. That is dread of extinction, fear of pain, and desire for happiness. In short, the adequate explanation of sympathy is to be found rooted back in reverence for life.

But let us inquire into this sympathy more closely. On what foundations does it exist? What is its natural explanation? To answer these questions, let us ask ourselves how we can live the life of another being in our own lives. In part, we depend upon the knowledge received through our senses. We see others; we hear them; we may touch them or be touched by them. And we may then engage in activities to help them. In other words, there is a natural, physical aspect to the matter which anyone must recognize. But what compels all this?

The important thing is that we are part of life. We are born of other lives; we possess the capacities to bring still other lives into existence. In the same way, if we look into a microscope we see cell producing cell. So nature compels us to recognize the fact of mutual dependence, each life necessarily helping the other lives which are linked to it. In the very fibers of our being, we bear within ourselves the fact of the solidarity of life. Our recognition of it expands with thought. Seeing its presence in ourselves, we realize how closely we are linked with others of our kind. We might like to stop here, but we cannot. Life demands that we see through to the solidarity of all life which we can in any degree recognize as having some similarity to the life that is in us.

No doubt you are beginning to ask whether we can seriously mean that such a privilege extends to other creatures besides human beings. Are they, too, compelled by ethics? I cannot say that the evidence is always apparent as it may be in human instances. But this I can say, that wherever we find the love and sacrificial care of parents for offspring (for instance) we find this ethical power. Indeed, any instance of creatures giving aid to one another reveals it. Moreover, there are probably more proofs than we might at first think. Let me tell you of three instances which have been brought to my attention.

The first example was told to me by someone from Scotland. It happened in a park where a flock of wild geese had settled to rest on a pond. One of the flock had been captured by a gardener, who had clipped its wings before releasing it. When the geese started to resume their flight, this one tried, frantically but vainly, to lift itself into the air. The others, observing his struggles, flew about in obvious efforts to encourage him; but it was no use. Thereupon, the entire flock settled back on the pond and waited, even though the urge to go on was strong within them. For several days they waited until the damaged feathers had grown sufficiently to permit the goose to fly. Meanwhile, the unethical gardener, having been converted by the ethical geese, gladly watched them as they finally rose together and all resumed their long flight.

My second example is from my hospital in Lambaréné. I have the virtue of caring for all stray monkeys that come to our gate. (If you have had any experience with large numbers of monkeys, you know why I say it is a virtue thus to take care of all comers until they are old enough or strong enough to be turned loose, several together, in the forest — a great occasion for them and for me!) Sometimes there will come to our monkey colony a wee baby monkey whose mother has been killed, leaving this orphaned infant. I must find one of the older monkeys to adopt and care for the baby. I never have any difficulty about it, except to decide which candidate shall be given the responsibility. Many a time it happens that the seemingly worst-tempered monkeys are most insistent upon having this sudden burden of foster-parenthood given to them.

My third example was given to me by a friend in Hanover, who owned a small cafe. He would daily throw out crumbs for the sparrows in the neighborhood. He noticed that one sparrow was injured, so that it had difficulty getting about. But he was interested to discover that the other sparrows, apparently by mutual agreement, would leave the crumbs which lay nearest to their crippled comrade, so that he could get his share, undisturbed.

So much, then, for this question of the natural origin of the ethic of reverence for life. It does not need to make any pretensions to high titles or noble-sounding theories to explain its existence. Quite simply, it has the courage to admit that it comes about through physiological makeup. It is given physically. But the point is that it arrives at the noblest spirituality. God does not rest content with commanding ethics. He gives it to us in our very hearts.

This, then, is the nature and origin of ethics. We have dared to say that it is born of physical life, out of the linking of life with life. It is therefore the result of our recognizing the solidarity of life which nature gives us. And as it grows more profound, it teaches us sympathy with all life. Yet, the extremes touch, for this material-born ethic becomes engraved upon our hearts, and culminates in spiritual union and harmony with the Creative Will which is in and through all.

— "The Ethics of Reverence for Life,"
in *Christendom,* 1936

On Life and Death

It is the number-one question about life: Where do you stand with regard to death?

If, in our thoughts, we are comfortable with death, then we accept each week, each day as a gift, and only when we allow life to be given to us in such a way, bit by bit, does it become truly precious.

— From a sermon preached at St. Nicolai's Church,
November 17, 1907

Epilogue

Let us conclude with an extract from a talk Schweitzer gave to Swiss and Alsatian helpers of his hospital in the summer of 1959, before they went to Lambaréné. With charm and a total lack of pomposity it brings to lighthearted life the problems, the crises, and the endless grinding toil of running the hospital, and makes of it quiet entertainment. One might see in it what Schweitzer meant when he said that one of the effects of Reverence for Life was that it made one both serious and (in the old sense) gay. And one can imagine how such a personality was able to dominate the many other strong personalities involved in operating the hospital:

In history, every schoolboy can tell when modern times started; in regard to the hospital I, too, can determine this pretty accurately.

Modern times at the hospital started in the year 1958. I will tell you how. The year before I had made a vow that no one would ever persuade me to build again. We had enough space and did not need any new buildings. I really thought that I was old enough to say sincerely: "I will not build any more. I have no one to help me with such things anyway. Therefore, all that's finished." This was a nice thought for me, but it worked out differently, because very strange things happened.

I first had to face the fact that we needed some space to store petroleum for our generators, and it had to be stored a good distance from living quarters in case it should be struck by lightning and start a fire. So I decided to build near the garden, away from our houses, a room where we would store oil and petrol.

But I said to myself: "This is only a little diversion. My vow of not building still holds." So I was getting set to start that when something else happened. An engineer from Zürich offered to build me a house, a prefabricated house made of aluminum.

First I thought, what would we do with aluminum? But the fellow finally convinced me that the house would be good for us and that it would be good for everybody to find out what experience one can have with aluminum in the tropics. So I told him: "Yes, and thanks."

Then they said: "You know, of course, you only have to make the foundation, but that is a trifle." Then they gave me the blue-prints. Just to read them was a nightmare for me. I am so used to building without plans. But then they told me that the foundation did not have to fit to the exact millimeter. Some story that was! If I'd not had a doctor who was knowledgeable about construction, I would have had to give up the thing at the start. But I had to work at that foundation for weeks and weeks. I who swore never to build again!

So this became building project number two, and I have to admit that the building was important because I did not really have enough space for all my patients. We have about three hundred and fifty couchettes, or mats covered with straw and a blanket. On these they sleep well enough, but there aren't enough of them. Because we have so many patients, I decided to agree to that aluminum building. This is the one that has worried me most and completing it has taken months. But when I left Africa, all was going well, and a fortnight ago I got the message that it is finished. How well an aluminum building fares in the tropics we shall soon see.

Now to building number three. I could ask you to guess what I might be referring to, and no one would. Could you imagine what else we would need in Lambaréné? No one knows? Well, I did not know it either. A building for an automobile, a Mercedes-Benz truck weighing five and a half tons, imagine that! How did such a thing come about, and why?

You might think that we got high-hatted, that the hospital became big and that we got proud and modern, but those who know me know that the danger of my becoming too modern is not great. But necessity stepped in, namely, the problem of feeding the hospital patients and of being sure that we always had enough to eat; we have to have twenty-seven tons of rice on hand in advance, because there may be months when no shipment comes from Saigon. At least that was always my working principle, to have that much rice on hand.

But suddenly in the year 1958, no rice is forthcoming. I asked in Lambaréné: "What is this? No rice has come. Are there no ships bringing rice from Saigon?" They answered me: "Oh, be calm, Monsieur. It will come. This is Africa. Don't worry. It will come. You must have patience. It does not come just when you wish, but it will come." So I kept my patience, as they had advised. Oh, yes. But one sack of rice was eaten up and then another and another and another. Finally I said, "What is this? We have only enough left for another week. What will happen?" So I went again to the officials in Lambaréné, and again they answered: "Don't worry. It will come. It will come."

But I'd heard enough of that. No, I thought, this is a time when more exact information is needed, and I found out that through political circumstances the rice traffic had been interrupted. Saigon had left the business pact with France, and did not accept payments in French money any more. It wanted dollars. You can imagine that we did not have too many dollars around. Anyway, we could not count any more on a regular supply from Saigon. The day had come when I had to admit that I had not enough food for my people. What could I do?

I went to the local administrator and said: "Listen. I have no more food for my people. I want to give up my hospital. Half of my patients I will send away and the other half I will bring to you, and you must feed them and care for them." This did it. The man finally understood what it all meant and he answered: "What can we do, cher Docteur?" Then I replied that the only alternative was for him to put a car at my disposal so that I could get to villages and buy bananas for my people. He said: "But certainly, of course, absolutely, Docteur." And he finally sent a car. So we had to change our staple from rice to bananas, a very serious thing.

How does the banana market operate in the tropics? In the old times, while the hospital was small, we had almost enough bananas. They were delivered to us by river-way. But not from down the river, only from up the river. This is because one cannot expect the men to paddle upstream with a heavy load of bananas. They can paddle back upstream after unloading the bananas. But with this system we were not getting enough bananas.

Then the Government built a road linking Libreville and Lambaréné because they also need bananas from the villages, where there are lots of plantations. One cannot expect the *indigènes* to carry bananas on the paths through the jungle to the Lambaréné hospital, because bananas are very heavy. Another disadvantage is that they spoil quickly and so cannot be stored for long. In fact, after four days in the tropics they start to rot. So I stood facing the problem, "How can I get hold of enough bananas quickly and steadily?"

After a week my great friend, the administrator, decided that I had used his car long enough. He said that he needed it for other projects. My luck had run out. But there was an *indigène* who did have a car and I told him I would make an agreement with him. I said: "On Thursday you drive from the hospital about twenty miles to those villages which sell bananas. I will send a nurse along with you. She will take along a scale to weigh the bananas, and help you load and unload!" That was fine, he told me, and so we made a contract. But one thing I forgot — to examine the car.

European people from Lambaréné came to me and said, "Docteur — How can you send your nurses off in a car which may burst into flames at any moment? It is a dangerous thing, and how its brakes ever work not even the Good Lord knows." I also realized that no such car would ever solve the problem permanently since we now required eight tons of bananas a week. What we obviously needed was a truck. But the road was not strong enough for a truck, so we also needed a new road. And a road that would even hold after heavy rains. At that point the connecting link to the government road was only a narrow path: moreover, it mounted to a steep hill.

So I had to build a road, and that turned out to he one of my biggest adventures. I even confessed to myself: "This you can't do." And in truth it was most unlikely that I could ever finish it because the road had to be widened about two and a half meters, and the foundation had to be filled in to about one meter, and the earth had to he carried by my good workmen.

But they are not favorably inclined to shovel tons of earth. Not very enthusiastic, at first they had to carry heavy earth for about half a kilometer, and the soil was wet besides. So you can see the beginning was one of the most difficult performances I started in Lambaréné. At first the *indigènes* really did not want to cooperate. We also had to hew the stones out of the ground, carry them to the road, and stones that were too big we had to crush with a hammer. I told myself: "Now, I, myself, will have to stand for at least four months to supervise this job." I who promised myself never to build again! I who had vowed to do only the hospital work from now on!

But at this point a miracle happened, a genuine miracle. A Volkswagen appeared on the horizon. Now a Volkswagen has a good reputation. Half of the cars that travel through the Sahara are Volkswagens. It's one of the few cars that can travel through sand. Anyway, from this Volkswagen four youths from Hamburg emerged, one of them slightly injured from an accident in a ditch. We took good care of him, and his companions walked through the hospital, looking very interested. They watched us work, and it was not long before they said to me: "Docteur, we have seen how hard you work, and we've decided to stay a while and help you build that road."

They took the tools and started to hew the big stones from morning till night, and the ambition of these German fellows had a most infectious effect on the *indigènes*. They became different people and started to work, as though it were fun. The spark took, and in three months we finished that road. It is a great road, sweeping behind the hospital in a big turn, and it rises to a hill of about thirty meters, and it serves well. Now the big question was, What kind of automobile would be most useful? I held a meeting of mechanics and asked them. Unanimously, they replied: "A Mercedes-Benz, five-and-a-half-ton diesel."

"Perhaps that is right," I thought. I had just read a report that the President of the French Republic and the German Chancellor had embraced each other at a political meeting, so I figured the time was ripe to buy a German car even if living in a French territory.

You see how wonderful it is when two people suddenly start up a friendship which no one would have expected! Anyway, I was lucky again. I contacted the Mercedes firm, and they delivered me the truck for a truly Christian price, I must say.

And so all is in order. The truck travels well on the new road; once a week it brings us about eight tons of bananas. Thus we've become independent of the arrival of rice. I need rice only for the summer months when bananas are more scarce. So fifteen tons of rice suffice. And that is how my hospital has entered into the modern age. But one thing I will guarantee you — modern times will not alter the old spirit of modesty and economy, the spirit of small beginnings. In this spirit the hospital developed, and in this spirit it shall live on.

— From Erica Anderson,
Albert Schweitzer's Gift of Friendship

Bibliography

By Albert Schweitzer

Albert Schweitzer — Hélène Bresslau, The Years Prior to Lambaréné, Correspondence 1902–1912. Trans. Antje Bultmann Lemke. Syracuse, N.Y.: Syracuse University Press, 2000.

Civilization and Ethics. Trans. C. T. Campion and C. E. B. Russell. *The Philosophy of Civilization*, part 2. London: A. & C. Black, 1923; New York: Macmillan, 1929, 1950.

"The Conception of the Kingdom of God in the Transformation of Eschatology." Epilogue to E. N. Mozley, *The Theology of Albert Schweitzer for Christian Inquirers* (London: A. & C. Black, 1950).

"Un culte du dimanche en forêt vierge." In *Cahiers Protestants* no. 2 (March 1931).

The Decay and Restoration of Civilization. Trans. C. T. Campion. *The Philosophy of Civilization*, part 1. London: A. & C. Black, 1923. New York: Macmillan, 1932, 1950.

From My African Notebook. Trans. C. E. B. Russell. London: George Allen and Unwin, 1938; New York: Henry Holt, 1939.

Un grand musicien français: Marie Joseph Erb. Strasbourg and Paris: Editions le Roux et Cie. Trans. in Joy, *Music in the Life of Albert Schweitzer*.

Indian Thought and Its Development. Trans. C. E. B. Russell. London: Hodder and Stoughton, 1936. Boston: Beacon Press, 1936. Reissued by A. & C. Black, 1951.

J. S. Bach. 2 vols. Trans. Ernest Newman, with alterations and additions at Schweitzer's request, from the German edition of 1908. Leipzig: Breitkopf und Härtel, 1908; London: Breitkopf und Härtel, 1911. Reissued by A. & C. Black, 1923; New York: Macmillan, 1949.

J. S. Bach, Le musicien-poète. French ed. Paris: Costallat, 1905. Leipzig: Breitkopf und Härtel, 1908. Trans. in part by Charles R. Joy and reprinted in Joy, *Music in the Life of Albert Schweitzer* (New York: Harper, 1951).

Memoirs of Childhood and Youth. Trans. C. T. Campion. London: George Allen and Unwin, 1924; New York: Macmillan, 1931.

More from the Primeval Forest. Trans. C. T. Campion. London: A. & C.
   Black, 1931; New York: Macmillan, 1948.
Music in the Life of Albert Schweitzer. Ed. Charles R. Joy. New York:
   Harper, 1951.
My Life and Thought. Trans. C. T. Campion. London: George Allen and
   Unwin, 1933; New York: Henry Holt, 1948. Quotations taken from
   the paperback edition, London: Unwin Books, 1966.
The Mystery of the Kingdom of God. Trans. Walter Lowrie. London:
   A. & C. Black, 1914; New York: Dodd, Mead, 1914; New York:
   Macmillan, 1950. Edition used here: A. & C. Black, 1956.
The Mysticism of Paul the Apostle. Trans. William Montgomery, B.D.
   London: A. & C. Black, 1931; New York: Henry Holt, 1931;
   Macmillan, 1955.
On the Edge of the Primeval Forest (Zwischen Wasser und Urwald).
   Trans. C. T. Campion. London: A. & C. Black, 1922; New York:
   Macmillan, 1948.
Paul and His Interpreters. Trans. William Montgomery, B.D. London:
   A. & C. Black, 1912; New York: Macmillan, 1912.
"Peace or Atomic War." Three broadcast talks transmitted on April 28,
   29, and 30, 1958; London: A. & C. Black, 1958. New York: Holt
   Rinehart and Winston, 1958.
The Quest of the Historical Jesus. Trans. William Montgomery, B.D. Lon-
   don: A. & C. Black, 1910; New York: Macmillan, 1945. Edition used
   here, 3rd ed. A. & C. Black, 1954.
"Religion in Modern Civilization." Two articles summarizing Schweit-
   zer's Hibbert Lectures given in the autumn of 1934. Printed in the
   Christian Century (November 21 and 28, 1934).
Reverence for Life. London: SPCK Press, 1966. Selection of sermons
   translated and edited by Ulrich Neuenschwander from *Strassburger
   Predigten* (Strasbourg sermons). Munich: Verlag C. H. Beck, 1966.

Other Works

Anderson, Erica. *Albert Schweitzer's Gift of Friendship.* New York: Har-
   per & Row, 1964.
————*The Schweitzer Album: A Portrait in Words and Pictures.* Addi-
   tional text by Albert Schweitzer. New York: Harper & Row, 1965;
   London: A. & C. Black, 1965.
Pierhal, Jean. *Albert Schweitzer: The Life of a Great Man.* London:
   Lutterworth, 1956.